there's a snake in my garden

JILL BRISCOE

ZONDERVAN
PUBLISHING HOUSE

OF THE ZONDERVAN CORPORATION | GRAND RAPIDS. MICHIGAN 49506

The poem "Father, Hear Us, We Are Praying" by Amy Carmichael from *Towards Jerusalem* is used by permission of The Society for Promoting Christian Knowledge, London, England.

To STUART — who keeps my mind on the Lord,
my feet on the ground, and my
heart in his love.

Contents

Preface

When one has enjoyed two people as we have enjoyed Stuart and Jill Briscoe, and been helped by their biblical ministry as we have been helped, I was more than interested to read something about their own spiritual pilgrimage. Being a woman, I wanted to know more about this remarkable woman and what makes her tick. I expected something honest, humorous, inspirational, and challenging. It was all that and more.

— RUTH B. GRAHAM

"The serpent was the craftiest of all the creatures the Lord God had made."
— Genesis 3:1, *Living Bible*

The Snake

Did you ever hear of Satan — or are you an unbeliever?
Did you ever laugh deridingly and prove him archdeceiver?
Did you ever hear of Calvary and shrug —
  "Why should I care"?
Did you ever care that God's *one* Son was mutilated there?
Did you ever see an empty cross and face an empty tomb?
Did you know He rose the *victor* o'er the snake and
  hell and doom?
Did you ever join His army, did you ever take your shield?
Did you ever march out sword in hand onto the battlefield?
Did you ever find the ranks grow thin the worse the
  fight became?
Did you ever watch men in retreat: the blind, the halt,
  the lame?
Did you ever notice nearer Christ the arrows thicker land?
Did you ever see the impact in His side, His feet, His hand?
Did you ever fully realize that Christ died without
  protection?
That you may have His armor, not act traitor by
  defection?
Did you ever wonder *why* He waits and tolerates
  lukewarmness?
And your pitiful rebellion and your coldness and your
  hardness?
And your casual indifference and your hunger for
  possessions?
Did you know He stops the arrows by his *constant
  intercessions*?
Did you ever thank your Jesus, did it ever break your
  heart?
Did you ever go out fighting and decide to play your part?
If you ever get around to war and put your armor on,
Then the snake will be defeated to the glory of God's Son.

1

Behind the Smile

I always believed in God, that Jesus Christ was His Son, and that the Bible was true. My parents taught me the difference between right and wrong. Right was being "good," which would make me and everyone else happy; wrong was being "bad," which would make me and everyone else sad. Why, then, did I find myself wanting to be bad instead of good? Why did wrongdoing bring me enjoyment? Why was being "good" dull and boring? Maybe someone had given me the wrong information.

Everything in my garden was lovely. Any legitimate tree was mine to enjoy: the tree of education; the tree of recreation; the tree of travel; the trees of fine friendships and wholesome entertainment; the precious trees

of a loving family and carefree days. Of these I freely
ate. But like Eve, I found myself desiring to possess
above all others the fruit from the one tree I was forbidden to touch!

As for Eve, so for me. The forbidden tree stood
among the forest of permitted things. Daily it reminded
me of one of God's choicest gifts to human beings
created in His image — the gift of my free will.

I didn't know it then, but along with the trees in my
garden there was also a snake. He came to me as he came
to Eve — in familiar form — for his devices have never
changed. He spoke to me through people I'd known all
my life, my friends who lived in the garden, too, so I
was not alarmed or suspicious.

"Eat the fruit. We have, and we didn't drop dead!"
So I took it, too, because I had to know what it tasted
like. I didn't realize that the process of death begins with
the first bite; by the time the fruit is finished, you begin
to feel pretty sick.

I loved and respected my parents too much to hurt
them. But I felt they wouldn't understand my rational-
izing my sin and calling it "growing up." So I decided
the best thing to do was to pretend to be "good" when
they were around. Meanwhile, I learned to eat my fruit
in parts of the garden inhabited only by the snake
and myself!

For example, I knew I shouldn't read dirty books, so
I didn't. But dirty thoughts were better and could be
indulged in behind the smile. I'd been told it was wrong
to cheat at exams, but I could dispense with my guilt
by arguing that cheating made for better grades, and
better grades for happier parents — as long as I wasn't
caught! But what if I was? Well then, I could always
chloroform my conscience and lie myself out of the situation. Wouldn't that be kinder than telling the truth,
which would cause hurt and embarrassment to those
I loved?

By now I was eighteen and becoming increasingly

confused. I was definitely not fulfilled. Something or
someone was still missing. I looked around at others.
Had they discovered the secret of life? Sometimes I got
behind their smiles and saw reality. One of the wealth-
iest men I knew committed suicide. Material things obviously hadn't helped him fill the void. My sick friend
in the hospital wasn't happy, but she blamed her health
problem. I had my health, so that wasn't the answer
either. Another friend wasn't satisfied, tossed to and fro
as she was between parents with marriage problems. Yet
living as I was in the midst of love, generated by my
parents' happy marriage, I still knew insecurity.

Somehow I sensed that the answer lay not in material
things or even in the enjoyment of the good things in
life such as health and happiness, but somewhere in the
mystical, moral realm — the "good" and the "bad" bit!
But goodness seemed so hard to define, and badness had
begun to make me sick of myself, so where was the
answer? What did I have to do? Where did I have to
go? How good did I need to become, or how bad did
I have to be to find — what? In my confusion, I didn't
know what I was looking for. Maybe "it" was waiting
for me in another garden, a new environment.

My chance came to prove the point when I was accepted at a teachers' training college at Cambridge.

"Yes," I assured the interviewer, "I love little children," while behind the smile the snake snickeringly
hissed, "You do?!"

Once established at college, the snake's cynicism
proved correct. Little children were soon categorized in
my mind as so much necessary nuisance value. They
made demands on my precious, trivia-filled time that I
needed for my headlong rush to find new trees laden
with fruit I had never dared to taste in my beautifully
protected garden back home.

I majored in drama and art, which helped me to
project the smile and perform whatever role it suited
my selfish interest to play. Many women have natural

abilities in this direction to begin with. Speech is a constant part of their existence, and drama helps to make them the stimulating, or more often aggravating, inveterate role players that they can be. I was apparently good at both, expecting others to be as impressed with my performance as I was! My life now became like one long "play," in every sense of the word. Before the curtains drew back and revealed me, I was alone, frightened, unsure of how I would relate to the crowd. Would they like the things I did? Would they laugh at my lines, cry at the pathos, and applaud my wild attention-getting antics? It was terribly important to me to know that I'd pleased them. Back in the dressing room with the make-up off, the costumes laid aside, what exhaustion, depression, and unfulfilled feelings were mine.

Perhaps there had been too many performances, or maybe I had just eaten too much bad fruit. I didn't know. Anyway, a mysterious stomach ailment took me into the hospital. Behind the smile I was terrified. I needed answers to my questions now. No longer was my major concern to fill a selfish life or get my own way, but how to deal with fear, cope with pain, look at the suffering of others and find a relevant comforting word. I had to grapple with the reality of death and find an answer.

I discovered that when I was flat on my back, there was only one way to look. Up! That's where I'd always believed God was to be found. But what do you say to a stranger who may not even be aware of the infinitesimal smudge of a mess lying in an obscure pinprick of a hospital bed on planet Earth?

"Help!" I said. "Make me better. Get me out of here! Quick, stop the pain. Are You receiving me?" O dear, that made Him sound like a radio. Radio or not, He picked up the message and placed a great transmitter next to my left ear.

Her name was Jenny, and she lay in the bed next to mine. She it was who told me that I had a snake in my garden, that I'd listened to his every word and believed his lies instead of God's truth. The fruit looked so good that I'd eaten it. I'd wanted to be wise and had finished up conceited and arrogant. I'd been my own god, but now I couldn't even answer my own prayers! No wonder I was sick in soul. My sin found me wearing fig-leaf arguments, carefully stitched but painfully inadequate.

"Jesus came and died on the cross for you, Jill," Jenny told me. "There He bruised the serpent's head and defeated him, but not before the snake had bruised His heel so that He suffered dreadfully. He rose again triumphant over death and sin and is alive. He wants to come into your life by His Holy Spirit."

"What's His Holy Spirit?" I asked. I had heard of the Holy Ghost, but His name had conjured up a picture of a sheet-shrouded spook who haunted old English churches! In my ignorant opinion He was left free so to do because evidently God had either died or gone on holiday, leaving behind His ghostly janitor. Jenny laughed. Did Christians laugh? I thought they were far too morbid and dreary and pious for that! But apparently I was wrong.

"The Holy Spirit was His divine nature released at Pentecost," she explained. "The Holy Spirit makes it possible for you to possess the very life of Christ."

The smile forgotten, tears flowed, as exposed in my garden and convicted of my sin I accepted God's covering for my nakedness. Clothed in His forgiveness and His grace I turned around to walk away from the tree of disobedience to a new life.

The snake in my garden writhed in fury and slithered out of sight — for a while!

2

The Shiniest Locker in the Ward

My bedside locker boasted the shiniest top in the hospital ward. Jenny had begun to "follow me up," and polishing my locker top was a good excuse for the Christian nurses on the ward to visit me! A pretty dark-haired nurse with twinkling blue eyes (Were Christians as pretty as this? I'd thought they were all dowdy, bunbedecked, long-skirted frumps!) asked me brightly, "Did something important happen yesterday?" Another girl inquired, "You're looking happy today. How's that?" While yet another took a much more direct approach, "Jenny says that you have something to tell me!"

I didn't know it, but Jenny was making sure I got plenty of practice giving my testimony! I had never heard of such a thing or read the verse in the Bible that

says, "If thou shalt confess with thy mouth the Lord
Jesus, and shalt believe in thine heart that God hath
raised him from the dead, thou shalt be saved" (Romans
10:9). But Jenny had knowledge of it and knew the
value of confession.

What did I have to confess after two days? About
the only thing I could say was that Jesus was Lord instead of me. That much I knew. I had asked Him into
my life to rule and to direct, and I knew He was there.
How did I know? Was it a feeling? No, it was deeper
than a feeling, bigger than an emotion; it was an inner
conviction. I was convinced with inner certainty that I
belonged to Jesus and that He belonged to me. As the
Bible says in Romans 8:16, "The Spirit itself beareth
witness with our spirit, that we are the children of
God," and it was God's Spirit telling my spirit that He
had arrived.

What did I have to tell after two days? I could tell
these new friends that I knew I'd been forgiven. I tried
to tell the dark-haired little nurse, but it was hard to
find the words. The love and gratefulness and tears kept
getting in the way! There had been so much to forgive.
"He that is forgiven much loves much," she said quietly.
"That's what Jesus said." She was right. To my amazement I loved Him already, and love for these new
friends overwhelmed me, too. I was so glad to learn I
wasn't the only one in the world who needed forgiveness and a new birth. There were others who had experienced the same thing. How many of them were there?

I lay in bed that night thinking back to the girls in
college. Suddenly I began to understand those students
with a special light in their eyes, spring in their step,
and wholeness of life. Later I learned it was holiness.
For so long they had mystified me and made me feel
uneasy. But now I understood them — they were Christians. How could I go back and expect them to accept
me? Especially that one girl I had taken delight in embarrassing in that drama production when my part had

involved so much blasphemy and innuendo, and she had had to respond. And then there was that senior student. I thought about the day I had so rudely burst into her room with a message and found her on her knees. She wasn't even embarrassed to be discovered looking so stupid praying beside her bed like a baby. I was the one who felt awkward and annoyed with her!

Then I must face my friends. Late into the night I lay thinking about them. What were they going to say? I thought I knew the answer to that. They would say what I would have said if the roles had been reversed. How could I answer their questions if they ever gave me the opportunity of answering them? I didn't even have a Bible.

The next morning I found a new Bible lying on my highly polished locker top. Eager, loving friends had bought it for me. I knew the answers I needed were contained inside, but I did wish it was a little smaller! It seemed so prominent perched there in full view of the ward. Ashamed of my ingratitude, I determined not to care. In fact, I decided I would leave it in full view when my friends came to visit me. However, my courage departed abruptly when I saw them swinging noisily down the ward in my direction, and I hastily covered it up with a magazine. Jenny sent one of her nurse friends over to meet my friends. The nurse removed the magazine, saying casually, "Can I borrow this for Jenny?" I knew Jenny didn't want to read it; she was helping me tell my friends. Now they saw it. They would have had to be suffering from a severe case of glaucoma to avoid doing so! The conversation became a little awkward. Sidelong glances were exchanged, and with stilted wishes for my recovery they took their leave.

"Jenny, I'll lose them," I lamented.

"What sort of friends are they if they ditch you because you've found God?" she asked me. "Anyway, if you do lose them, God will give you new friends."

"But I don't want new friends. I want my old ones.

Does being a Christian mean I'll have to stop doing things with them and stop going to the places I'm used to going to? What will I have to give up?"

I'll never forget her answer. "God will only ask you to give up those activities and habits that are going to do you harm, and you'll know what those things are. He'll tell you."

"How will He tell me, Jenny?, I don't know what I should or shouldn't do. I don't know where or where not to go. I don't know *anything!*"

"Here you are in the hospital. You think you have been laid aside by illness, but you haven't. You've been called aside for stillness. So, get your nose in this Bible and start."

"But how? Where do I start, and what do I read? How will I understand and know I'm interpreting it correctly?"

"Jesus said, 'The Holy Spirit will guide you into all truth.' He'll take His Word and make it make sense to you. Start in the New Testament with the Gospel of John."

She dug into a big purse hanging on the end of the bed and produced numerous booklets which she gave me to read. Two by the Reverend J. R. W. Stott, *Becoming a Christian* and *Being a Christian*, explained simply just what had happened to me and encouraged me to seek to grow as a baby Christian by desiring the "sincere milk of the word" (1 Peter 2:2).

"Now then, you're going to need to start having a quiet time," Jenny announced.

I eagerly agreed! The sound of the battle ahead convinced me I needed to escape from my responsibilities and my problems to some cave of solitude. But apparently "escape" was not the idea behind a "quiet time." The idea was to open one's ears to the still, small voice that would keep asking the simple question, "What doest thou here?" The owner of the voice would listen to all my excuses and then command me to depart from my

cave into the battle, fortified and encouraged by my
time alone with Him.

"Start with fifteen minutes a day," I was instructed.
"Read a portion of the Bible; these notes will help you,"
she said, giving me some daily Bible helps. "Then pray
about what you read. Look for commands to obey,
promises to claim, warnings to heed, and answers to your
questions. At the end of your daily time with God, start
learning these verses." Then she handed me a little
packet put out by The Navigators with verses of Scripture to memorize printed out on little cards.

"There are forty-eight in each packet. I'll listen to
them as you learn them!" Then she produced three
large books from somewhere under her bedcovers. "Read
these in your spare time. They are adventure stories of
people who became Christians and went about turning
the world upside down." My shiny locker top had disappeared under a pile of books, booklets, and Bible. I
thought of the "called aside for stillness" and the "quiet
time" and smiled at the irony of the terms! But I got the
message. I'd better get to work.

During the remaining days in the hospital I read the
story of Daniel. The story of the lions' den was not
news to me, but the story of Daniel refusing to eat the
king's meat was! As I read the story in one of my first
quiet times, the Holy Spirit took the truth and applied
it. "Jill, I want you to purpose in your heart not to
defile yourself with the king's meat!" God was telling
me forbidden fruit was out. He was teaching me that
anything which would defile my relationship with the
Holy Spirit was not to be eaten. That if I would say
"no" when the time came to enter the den of lions (I
had an immediate vision of my friends with hairy manes
and wide mouths waiting to gobble me up!), God would
shut their mouths. And my God would prove Himself not
only to me, but also to others who might be watching.

When I talked to Jenny later about the friend problem, she said, "Of course you may win them to Christ, and then you won't lose them."

"Me?!"

"Yes, you!" said Jenny, ignoring my incredulity. "Jesus Christ is a great soul-winner, and He's come into your life to use your body as a ship from which to fish."

"Help!" I thought, wondering how long it would take the good Lord to discover I was more like a leaky sieve than a sturdy trawler.

As if she had read my thoughts, Jenny commented that God liked cracked, broken vessels best. That way He, the Great Fisherman, got the glory. She then showed me 1 Corinthians 1:26-29 and pointed out that as I was foolish, weak, base, and despised, I was just the vessel He was looking for! That was all right then. He would surely gain much glory by using me!

"How do I lead them to Christ?" I asked.

"Tell them what I told you," she said. "Use these verses: *Romans 3:23* — the fact of sin; *Romans 6:23* — the penalty of sin; *John 3:16* — Jesus died for sinners; *Revelation 3:20* — you must receive Him. Ask them if they believe this. If they say 'yes,' ask them if they know how to receive Him. If they answer in the negative, ask them if they would like you to help them by praying a prayer they could repeat and make their own, like the one we prayed together. Do you remember?"

I remembered. My memory wasn't as bad as that — it was only a week away! I wrote it down in the back of my Bible along with the Bible verses. I was getting my fishing equipment ready!

3

Let's Go Fishing

A few days later the intrepid fisherman, clutching her rod cautiously, approached the muddied streams of college where the "big fish" were to be found.

Jenny had been at it again! She had let the other Christian fishermen know I was on my way. To my amazement all sorts of strangers became my friends immediately, including the girl in the drama incident and the senior student at college! It was a whole new world. We shared the same life, the same goals, and the same commission. Jesus had said, "Come after me and I will make you fishers of men." I learned quickly that although we were doing the same thing, each of us had to catch our own fish. I could be excited at my sister's catch, but I could also expect a fish of my own, even though I was so new and inexperienced. (After all, little boys just starting out with a stick and a bent pin expect to catch something!)

Jenny had told me to make myself available to the Lord day by day and watch to see whose company I was thrown into. I was to listen for any stray remark I could use as an opportunity; then I could invite the one I believed God was bringing across my path to coffee and lead her to Christ! It sounded so easy. I prayed. I watched. I listened — expecting to be led to someone needing Jesus. Sure enough I was!

"Would you come to coffee tonight, Audrey?"

"Sure," she replied.

"Help, Lord! She accepted, now what?" I reported to the Big Fisherman.

God was good to me. Audrey was full of questions.

"Jill what's happened to you? Are you going to a nunnery or something?" With my heart beating wildly, I answered as best I knew how, read the verses to her, and asked her if she believed.

"Yes I do," she replied seriously.

Now came the big question, "Will you pray with me to accept Christ?" I couldn't ask it. What if it didn't work? How foolish we'd look. Maybe it was enough to influence her! I had an immediate picture of my father, an ardent salmon fisherman, announcing at the end of a day's fishing, "Well, I influenced a lot of fish today!" No, I knew I had to catch her. So I asked the all-important question, "Will you accept Jesus Christ as your Savior and Lord?"

"Yes," she replied. "Oh, Jill, yes."

We knelt; we prayed. I peeked between my fingers in hope and fear. What I saw convinced me that another miracle had happened. Triumphantly I paid my visit to Jenny with Audrey in tow. Instead of the expected congratulations, I received immediate orders!

Now that I had become a spiritual mother (and at such a young age too!), I had to take my responsibility seriously. My job was to feed the new spiritual baby by helping her to read the Bible and have a quiet time. I needed to protect her by prayer and encouragement. Then I could help her to lead another to Christ. After this I must see to it that she became a good spiritual parent, and so on ad infinitum!

The future stretched before me bright with promise. I had never experienced a thrill comparable to seeing heaven open to my friend Audrey. To watch one forgiven much and see her beginning to love much. To see how God began to answer my prayers and her prayers, changing lives, dissipating loneliness, giving purpose and direction. To be a blessing to those closest to me was thrilling. How I longed for everyone to know Him.

Most fishermen have many fish tales of "the one that got away!" My best friend was one such fish. We shared a room during our first year in college, and not wishing to embarrass her (that was my excuse!), I asked a Christian friend if I might have my quiet time in the sanctuary of her room. Never will I forget the day she firmly said, "Jill, you go to your own room and have it there!"

"Oh, but I can't," I protested as the door closed firmly and finally behind me. "Help, Lord, be reasonable," I complained. "I can't kneel and pray in front of her. She'll misunderstand and it won't help You at all!" The battle raged. I thought of Daniel praying three times a day with his window open even when he knew the opposition was peeking in — and that meant the lions! I wondered why he didn't shut the windows. Then I realized that was just what I had been doing — shutting the windows!

At last I knelt. I couldn't pray, but it didn't matter. It was enough to be there. Steps came along the corridor. I never realized before how short the corridor was! The door swung open. Silence. Unbelieving silence. Then a gasp as the door slammed and my friend retired to spread the news that she was living with a religious maniac. She never spoke to me again, even though we lived together for the rest of the year.

I complained to my Master about the oppressive silence.

"Well," said the Lord, "you prayed that I would shut the lion's mouth; now be satisfied!"

I understood my roommate's scorn and disgust. She knew me so well. She believed I had to be pretending, and this understandably was the height of hypocrisy.

I visited the hospital and poured out my distress to Jenny, who listened but gave me little sympathy. She renewed her simple challenge to me to let my life speak. She gave me assurance by sharing many of her tales of the "one that got away." Sometimes they ended up on another fisherman's rod, she said, so I was just to pray, commit my friend to Him, and let Him deal with the hurt.

Jenny's health improved. It was time for her to leave the hospital and me. I was glad she was well, but wished God would keep her around a little longer. Couldn't the Lord arrange a simple appendectomy or something? What would I do without her? But God knew I had her on a spiritual pedestal, and it was time to rely on Him alone — not on any prop, however precious.

"What happens if I fall?" I wailed.

"Oh, you'll fall!" she replied cheerfully. "What toddler doesn't? Just get up and try again. There's never been a healthy baby who hasn't learned to walk with practice!"

I remembered those words in the days that followed. Days after the first thrill had left me and I couldn't feel His presence, I remembered that a loving parent removes his support to teach his child to walk in obedience. That was a hard lesson, but I was growing up.

I returned to the hospital once more before they discovered my ailment and remedied it. There was a girl in the ward who had had the same serious bone operation that Jenny had had and who was in great pain. Being allowed to move around the ward, I longed to help. How? The idea came straight from heaven. Her locker top! I was there in a flash tidying it up, leaving her a booklet, soothing her brow, loving her already before she became my sister in Christ.

That night after she became a new person, I prayed, "I'm a leaky vessel, but thank You for coming on board, Captain. I'm a lousy fisherman, but keep up the lessons. I'm learning. Thank You for helping me to discover a gift — I can polish locker tops."

Bugs

Wouldn't it be lovely if a bug could stay always
Warm inside its silk cocoon, protected all its days
Alone in dark oblivion, no need to fly the skies?
Let's face it — God's rebellious world's no place for
    butterflies.

Now God, He made these little bugs and placed
    within *His life*
So growth, the natural evidence, brings strain and
    stress and strife;
For as she grows the cozy case becomes a prison
    strong,
The bug now knows she *must* break out; to stay a
    bug is *wrong*.

At last the struggle over — the butterfly is free
    to fly God's earth upheld by Him in matchless
    symmetry.
Cries watching man in God's lost world, "*A Miracle
    is this,*
From crumpled bug to butterfly" —
                    God's metamorphosis.

4

Arranged, Strange, or Deranged

Having graduated from college, I began teaching in my hometown of Liverpool. I taught first graders, loved my work, and had plenty of free time for the King's business. Someone said, "The mission field is between your own two feet." If that were true, part of my commission lay within the four walls of my classroom. First graders? Well, they surely needed a changed nature, sweet though they were! I never had to teach them to answer back, be rude, selfish, or stubborn; all that appeared to come quite naturally. I decided it would help if I had someone within their group on my side as I struggled to teach not only first steps of math and English, but also priorities of life.

My problem was that I was not the teacher He

wanted me to be, and for a simple reason: I could not control my temper. Fresh out of college and believing in the "new" concept of free choice, I sought to put into practice all I had learned. The basis of this concept was that the children should be free to choose exactly what they wanted to do. As learning comes through doing, they would learn more quickly by "choosing" to work at math and English instead of being "made" to do things they disliked.

"Now, children, math or art today?" I inquired in a cheerful voice. Paint brushes and easels ran out while I was left holding a pile of math materials. "Reading or the playhouse?" I made a mental note that we would need a new playhouse soon. Due to overcrowding it was due for demolition! "Watch the rabbits, stick bugs, and mice, children! Try not to step on them," I pleaded. "Johnny, did you try to teach Mickey Mouse to swim today? . . . What do you mean you had a burial service in the sandbox?"

The climax came one day when I discovered a game of hospital in progress. Some nice little boys were playing out their frustrations by taking out a friend's tonsils with a pair of scissors. Just as I made this discovery, a child tripped over the leg of a chair and fell against a paint easel, emptying pots of paint the entire length of the classroom. I felt if the children were allowed freedom to create as they wished, so was the teacher. I created — and how!

Later, at home, I knelt and asked forgiveness. This had to be beaten. How could I serve Him when there was a part of my life constantly being defeated? Was I supposed to live with defeat because I couldn't be perfect? I read the answer in Romans 6:14: "Sin shall not have dominion over you!" But it had!

How disappointed the Lord must be! Miserably I struggled to gain control over my temper at school. Day after day I returned defeated to pray the same prayer, "Forgive me, Lord, I did it again." If there was no victory in the Christian life, just what did Christ offer? If only I could feel He understood. But I had this foreboding that He stood in the corner of my classroom, loving the children, cross with me, and ready to rebuke and condemn the moment I transgressed.

At that time I read a story about a lighthouse keeper who broke a window in his lighthouse. Believing no ships were in the area, he filled in the aperture with a board. The light shone brightly from all sides except one. There was only one "part dark." Surely it wouldn't matter. That night a ship approaching the lighthouse on the dark side was shipwrecked. The moral: There must be no "part dark." I knew this. No matter how much His light was shining out of other areas of my life, this temper part was dark; it was tripping up those to whom I was seeking to witness at school. I was not to settle for defeat. This (I learned from my Bible) was not normal Christianity.

I searched the Scriptures for an answer. In Hebrews 4:15 I read that He "was in all points tempted like as we are, yet without sin!" If it said in *all* points, it meant in *all* points. In other words, He understood the pressure! He was not standing in the corner of my classroom waiting to condemn, but in the person of the Holy Spirit He had come alongside to help. In fact, He was saying, "Aren't they little beasts! How frustrating they are even though we love them so much! I understand. I stood among My children here on earth and watched the chaos created by freedom without discipline! You're going to need more patience than mere human patience, more love than you are capable of. Let Me give you Mine; for love, patience, and self-control are the products of My work within you." I needed to appreciate and appropriate those divine qualities.

Soon I learned to mix freedom with discipline, and drawing on His resources I knew victory at last. Many of those little children found the Savior and gave me good practice in breaking the Bread of Life small enough for them to digest. What a message we Christians have to give to the world! It is possible to have no "part dark."

Now I felt I should join a group of Christians and help them get the message out. I had so much to share about how Christ can overcome. But which group should I join? I began looking for a fellowship of believers. I discovered that Christians appeared to be divided into three categories: the arranged, the strange, or the deranged!

The *arranged* were just that. Religious routine rolled monotonously along taking them with it. These people usually sat in the same pew every week, wore hats to church, carried big Bibles, taught Sunday school, and cut up sandwiches for ladies' teas. Conforming to their physical image, I joined them. All my make-up was removed overnight, resulting in the most irritating inquiries as to the state of my health. My hair was cropped like a boy's to avoid vanity. It did! I lowered my skirts to regulation lengths, which had dangerous repercussions since I was driving a motor scooter at the time. I learned all the right choruses to sing at the after-church fellowship. This fellowship consisted of party games, which made me feel rather stupid having last played such games in the eighth grade. But this was apparently how Christians had fun. Then we had a few choruses (which also appeared rather childish) and a five-minute epilogue delivered in an apologetic manner, as if the person presenting the Word wished he didn't have to bring Christ into it. I observed that most of the young people left before the epilogue!

I was soon bored with it all. This wasn't getting the message out! Sunday after Sunday those of us who were saved listened to a message on how to be saved, while those who were lost continued unaware of their plight, far removed from the preacher's voice.

I looked around and decided to join the *strange* group! This group of Christians had decided that the arranged group was for the old fogies and not for "in-touch-with-the-Lord, go-ahead" folk like them! Bible texts poured from their lips. They rushed about on street corners giving out tracts. They were *determined* to be a blessing, and were always ready to tell you (with humility) how many drunks had accepted Christ through them last night, or how they had spent the whole night in prayer! They scoffed at established church services and sang hymns in public places even if they had voices that sounded like cinders grating under a door. Although I had some misgivings about many of the pushier parts of their outreach, I never dared to voice them in case I should be considered unspiritual.

I threw myself into the program. It was certainly exciting and a lot more fun than the arranged group! I learned how to reach the tough "Teddy boys" through street meetings. One of them even gave me his flick knife as a keepsake. I painted chairs and scrubbed floors at the Chinese Gospel Mission in a seedy part of downtown Liverpool. I preached from the precarious pulpit of a rowboat to people having picnics along the riverside and stood on upturned crates on bomb sites enjoying my first taste of open-air preaching. (This last activity was brought to an abrupt halt when my head teacher from school joined the crowd one night!) We raided coffee bars, formed rescue squads for sex parties, and marched among the crowds at the dog track with Bible placards.

I still attended church, but my heart was filled with pride. Just what did these poor dead Christians know about real Christianity? I refused to listen to the wise counsel of a dear couple who loved the Lord and me and who could see that my exhausting schedule was rapidly leading me to a nervous breakdown. They knew I was a candidate for group three, the *deranged* group. My wild career in group two finally ended after I got involved with a boy who was hiding from the police. I was trying to help him, but it was I who needed help, for the police believed I was an accessory after the fact to his many crimes.

Balance was a word I disliked; it sounded too much

like compromise to me. But balance was certainly just what I needed! I needed to stop conforming to a group and start discovering and developing my own gifts.

Perhaps what I needed was a husband to help me see myself as God and others saw me. But a Christian husband seemed as impossible a dream to me as a trip to Mars! There were few Christian men in fellowships at home, and those that were there seemed weedy, weak, or insipid! It didn't seem safe to ask the Lord to provide me with a husband, for He hadn't much to choose from. I was afraid He might present me with a balding, squint-eyed, spotty boy six inches shorter than me and say, "He's a great Christian; marry him!" No, it was obviously safer to forget all about marriage. I had proved over three years that God could satisfy me without a man in my life. So the obvious thing to do was head for Africa and become an intrepid missionary. There I could bury myself beneath a jungle hat and a mosquito net. With this noble intention in mind, I applied to Bible college! It was full, so they couldn't take me. I had no idea how Africa could possibly manage without me, but I decided to spend time seeking to disciple a wild group of teen-agers who had found Christ through the ministry of the strange group!

I found myself with eighty teens. They were new Christians, eager to learn all I could teach them. This didn't take long, so I looked around somewhat desperately for help. All the people I asked advised me to "take them away somewhere for a retreat!" (This reminded me of the story of the feeding of the five thousand. "Send them away," the disciples pleaded. But the Lord demanded that *they* give them to eat.) Perhaps the church had nothing to give — or were they afraid of the arranged getting deranged if the strange appeared in the church pew?

So away we went to a beautiful castle, Capernwray Hall, situated at the gateway to England's Lake District. It was a Christian youth conference center run by an organization called Torchbearers. I hadn't known such places existed. There was freedom with discipline, fun without frivolity — balance! Here I watched the gifted staff counsel and teach, encourage and train my young people. And here it was I met a man who was to balance me!

Stuart Briscoe was tall, dark, and handsome, so obviously he was a temptation sent by the devil to distract me from following the Lord! Never in those first days did it occur to me that God could give *me* a man like this. One evening while battling with my vulnerable heart, I read that Jesus sent His disciples out two by two!

"Don't tease me, Lord," I prayed. "You know my heart. You know I'm happy alone with You. So what's happening to me?" Then I read, "He that spared not his only Son, but delivered him up for us all, how shall he not with him also freely give us all things?" (Rom. 8:32).

I knew what would happen. I'd fall in love and then God would take him away and I'd get hurt.

"If your son asks for bread, do you give him a stone? Of course not," said the Father.

"But I don't deserve him, Lord!"

"He doesn't deserve *you!*" the Lord replied. "But you surely need someone to take you in tow! Step into My plan for your life, Jill. Category four is called the *pre-arranged*. Say 'thank you,' and let's have a wedding!"

We did, and then it was I who learned that weddings last a day, but marriage is forever.

5

It Is Not Good for Man to Live Alone

Asked to define a game of golf, a person rather cynically replied, "Golf is a good walk spoiled!" Maybe the man in question had just finished a bad round, or hadn't been trying very hard, or didn't feel it important enough to improve his game. He may have blamed the course, the equipment, or his partner. If he was really upset, he might have changed clubs and partner too!

To many people, marriage seems to be held in no higher regard than a game of golf! How sad, when marriage was intended by God to bring the greatest of human happiness to man. To any thinking person it is quite obvious that it's the bad golfer not the game of golf that's at fault. In the same way, it is not the divine institution of marriage that's at fault but the man and woman playing the course. If the rules are obeyed and the participants are willing to work at it, they might begin to enjoy their relationship.

One of the problems we face today is sheer ignorance of the rules. The biblical concept of marriage is so often untaught or is couched in churchy traditional terms (such as "holy matrimony") which usually do not relate to the everyday world of the young. Before I found Christ, I thought marriage was the wedding day. However, once I'd met Jesus and learned that marriage was forever, I decided I'd better find out how it worked!

Marriage, being God's idea, had to be good! Perhaps it was because marriage was His idea that He accepted in the person of Jesus Christ the invitation to the wedding at Cana in Galilee that we read about in John 2. As I wrote our wedding invitations to our relatives and friends, I sent one to heaven straight from my heart. It read, "The future Mr. and Mrs. D. S. Briscoe request the pleasure of the company of Jesus Christ at their wedding." I had an instant reply by air mail, "Delighted to accept!"

He was coming! How exciting! What would He do? Well — nothing — if He wasn't asked. I knew that from the Scriptures. The problem with the marriage at Cana seemed to be that He was invited as a mere guest, not as governor of the feast. The governor was the one who was in control, gave the orders, and was obeyed. I didn't want Christ to be a guest on the same level as my loved ones and friends — there merely to add a bit of religion to the scene. I did not want the wine of our love to run out nor our relationship to become insipid, colorless, and tasteless. I knew the secret lay in His preeminence as governor and our obedience to His commands. "Whatsoever he saith unto you, do it," (John 2:5) was the best wedding advice we'd heard anywhere. How foolish of us to buck the divine principles and do our own thing when the Bible taught that our joy (through obedience) would be better than anything we had experienced in our relationship before.

Now I discovered that the snake was still in my garden! He hadn't been absent between the end of chapter 1 and this point in my life; he'd just been slithering in and out and around. But never did I expect him to turn up as consistently as he did in our early days of married bliss! The snake hates any marriage that has the Lord God in control, walking and talking in the cool of the day with the two He made especially for each other and for Himself. God placed man in an ideal environment, but even in Paradise something was missing. "It is not good that the man should be alone," said God (Gen. 2:18); so He set "the solitary in families" (Ps. 68:6), and He started in Eden.

The first hissing suggestion I heard from the snake, as I happily washed, cooked, worked, and cared for our baby David in those early years of marriage, was the usual misquoting of Scripture for which the snake is renowned. Because it sounded familiar to me, I was taken off guard.

"It is not good for man to be alone," he hissed in my ear. "God never intended it, so why does that Christian husband leave you alone so much? He should be here to help you with the baby and the work instead of being busy with God's business!" Next time you hear the hiss of the snake, check up on his quote. I didn't. If I had, I would have remembered that the verse about being alone referred to the man and that the woman was created to help the man, not vice versa.

The fruit of self-pity looked good to me, so I ate it. It immediately created a desire in me to encourage my husband to eat it also.

"Why don't you stay home on the weekends and evangelize here?" I asked him. "Look over there outside that Cat's Whisker coffee bar across the street. All those young people need to hear the Gospel. Why preach to a dozen little old ladies in church?"

Now let me assure you — I couldn't have cared less about the needy young people across the street. I was simply using them as an excuse to get my own way. I was lonely, and so I was manipulating to get Stuart to obey me rather than God. And I was using a religious excuse to accomplish my purpose. How true is the Scripture that says, "The heart is deceitful above all things, and desperately wicked" (Jer. 17:9).

Looking out of our windows and across the street, my husband commented simply, "What do you think you are here for? You reach them."

A thousand excuses leapt to my lips. "My job is to be your wife and look after you and the baby while praying and supporting your ministry. I haven't time!"

"Well, you've more time than I have," he replied. "Jill, God doesn't ask you for your husband's time, or your child's time; He asks you for your spare time!" And with this he packed his case and was gone!

"Well," said the snake, "how unfair. Anyway, you can't go over there and talk to them. They're another generation. (I was 23 years old!) Get some teens to go!" This last was said with a smug hiss, as he knew the only Christians I'd met were very young in Christ, shy and nervous. Of course he'd forgotten the principle of 1 Corinthians 1:26-28, and therefore made a bad mistake.

Seeing a way out of my involvement, I accepted his advice and decided to invite three or four young people to do those things I didn't dare to do. I would stay home and pray for them (nice of me!) and make an English cup of tea (which is what you always do in times of crisis) in case they needed to retire from the battlefield to recuperate.

The Lord was about to teach me a lesson. It was the same lesson I began to learn at the beginning of this chapter. God leaned out of heaven and said to me, "Jill, you're right. It is not good for man to be alone or woman for that matter, especially if the man is called away to be about his Father's business. I'm about to

rectify the matter and send you some company!" As my
three brave but quaking teens went across the road to
approach dozens of wild-looking youngsters outside the
coffee bar, the establishment was closed because of a
fight; my three well-trained evangelists panicked and invited everyone back across the street for a free cup of
English tea! Looking out of what I had believed was my
safe little cocoon, I discovered with horror that the time
had come for me to become a butterfly!

"There you are, Jill. We brought them!" my evangelists announced triumphantly. The kids streamed into
the house filling every room, chattering and kidding.

"Yes, you did!" I replied weakly. I heard the Lord
chuckle. I'm sure it was the Lord. I knew it wasn't the
snake as he wasn't in the mood for laughter! Late into
the night we talked and witnessed and argued and
prayed. Very near midnight my husband returned from
his preaching engagment, tried to get in, and couldn't!
Hearing Stuart's knock, a lanky youth with hair dyed in
different colored strips opened the door a crack and
muttered, "Sorry, mate, there's no room!"

It was a new beginning for both of us. My spare
time bulged with positive activity, while Stuart fought
his own battles with his heart about his involvement
with the teens. I sat down and made a note of my daily
routine and blocked off my spare time, setting it aside
for God. Young people were finding Christ, and follow-
up Bible studies began in our home. I thought back to
our beautiful wedding service and the text a preacher
had spoken from: "It was noised abroad that Jesus was
in the house." So it began to be, and the crowds came
until, like the Bible story, they could hardly get near
Him because of the "press." I prayed, "Oh my Lord,
may Your presence in our home be 'news' around town!"

I came to realize that even though I had committed
my life to Stuart, this did not mean I had committed my
relationship with God to Stuart! That was still my responsibility. Even though we could read and pray and

learn of Him together, even though God had a special plan for our lives collectively, I needed to fulfill His plan for my life individually! I needed to guard my own personal devotional time and not let collective devotions take that place. God had work for me to do — spiritual work in areas that my husband never would have had time or talent for.

Our home could be my fishing boat during his absence. Our baby could be a means of contact among other young mothers in the park or at the store. I had a commission from God not only to care physically and practically for my family's needs in a manner that would bring glory to Him, but also to bring the Gospel to every creature. I must not abdicate that responsibility just because I had gotten married!

So many legitimate excuses to fade off the spiritual scene were available in those happy days. As Martha, I was careful and troubled about good and necessary things, but I needed to remember Mary's better part — to sit at His feet and look in His face and listen to His word. And when I did that, I was continually reminded that two people made one must equal twice the impact for His Kingdom! As God's Word says, "One [of you will] chase a thousand, and two put ten thousand to flight" (Deut. 32:30).

6

The Trees of the Forest Will Clap

Six months after our ministry began among the young people outside the Cat's Whisker coffee bar, we began to experience an unsettling type of inner conviction. We felt we were being gently prepared for transfer!

Stuart was beginning to receive far more invitations for ministry than he was able to accept. His career offered many excellent opportunities that began to conflict with his Christian outreach, and the time had come to make a choice. Something had to go. Was it to be banking or the development of his ministry? We began to ask the Lord about it.

Guidance is a practical business. The will of God is that which lies immediately before us — the obvious, not the obscure. It had not been difficult to discern the will of God for our lives during the days that had passed. We needed to reach those lost young people on our doorstep. We didn't even need to pray about that! Prayer can be a wonderful excuse for not doing God's will. "Let's pray about it," we say, and settle for words instead of work. As God said to Joshua, "Get up off your face and go and do what I've told you to do. There is sin in the camp, and you know my principle about that. Go and put it right, and then come and pray" (Josh. 7:10, 11, author's paraphrase). In the same way, we don't need to pray about whether or not we should reach the lost; the principle has already been outlined. We shouldn't pray "Shall I go?" We should pray *as* we go!

But now a situation arose where the next obvious thing was not quite so obvious. We had come to a crossroads, and a choice had to be made between banking or preaching. As was usual in our relationship, I arrived far too rapidly at a decision and happily said to my husband, "You pray, I'll pack!" However, as the breadwinner and head of our home, Stuart needed to be absolutely sure he was doing the right thing before he turned down an excellent offer of promotion and twelve years' service in a secure profession. So we drew up a list of the principles of guidance we found in the Scriptures:

1. The advice of mature Christians
2. Our natural talents, abilities, and spiritual gifts
3. Inner conviction as we search the Scriptures for direction, separately and together
4. Circumstances involving practical considerations having to do with money, family commitments, etc.

We then began working our way through these directives. The men Stuart sought out for counsel unanimously advised us to leave banking. Stuart's ministry had been so developed and blessed by God that these godly men felt constrained to point him towards this decision. Next we began to search the Scriptures together, reading in the book of Matthew. There we found such verses

as "The harvest truly is plenteous, but the labourers are
few" (Matt. 9:37), and "Lay not up for yourselves
treasures upon earth, where moth and rust doth corrupt,
and where thieves break through and steal" (Matt. 6:19).
Very appropriate for us! While miles apart, both of us
were amazed to be individually impressed by the same
verse from the book of Isaiah which said, "Ye shall go
out with joy, and be led forth with peace: the mountains and the hills shall break forth before you into singing, and all the trees of the field shall clap their hands"
(Isa. 55:12). We had no idea why we felt so convicted
that this particular verse had relevance to our situation,
but we shared it and noted it down. Perhaps we would
be able to understand it later. Circumstances appeared to
point to full-time work as well. At exactly this point in
time, two missionary societies invited us to join them
without any manipulation on our part. We prayed about
our family commitments. To accept one of these opportunities would put us within a few miles of Stuart's
recently widowed and very lonely mother. As we pon-
dered this factor, that very morning we received a moving letter from her and our daily reading contained these
words spoken by Jesus from the cross, "Behold thy
mother!" (John 19:27).

As we made a list for and against all these possibilities,
Stuart became convinced he had to hand in his resignation to the bank. The next decision was the hardest.
Which of the two missionary societies should we
choose? The lists we had made concerning both societies
appeared equal, and we needed to give an answer within
three short weeks. We talked and prayed and searched
the Scriptures but seemed to be no nearer to a solution.
Then we asked God for a sign.

Both societies had discussed our roles, money, and all
other details; yet strangely enough, neither had men-
tioned accommodations.

"Let's ask the Lord to show us His will," Stuart said.
"Like Gideon, we'll put out a fleece." We determined

to choose whichever society offered us a house.

The night before our decision was required, the director of one of the societies came to us and spent a wonderful evening of fellowship and prayer. We listened hard all night. There was no mention of a house! It was incredible. Every detail had been talked over. We looked at each other as we shut the door behind this good servant of the Lord. There had been no offer of a house from the alternative work either. Had we made a mistake in asking for a sign? We had to give our decision the very next day. We turned to go upstairs to bed, and suddenly the phone rang. It was the leader of one of the societies ringing to apologize for phoning at such a late hour, but telling us he had foolishly forgotten to mention a rather important detail. The detail was "the offer of a house."

We laughed for joy, we packed, and we journeyed eighty miles up the freeway to England's beautiful Lake Country, where our work was to be. We arrived late on an April evening. The next day dawned bright and clear. The birds welcomed us with triumphant song, and we walked outside and gazed around the forest of trees about to burst forth in all their spring glory. Suddenly we remembered the verse we both had discovered a few months earlier! I ran into our new home and returned with my Bible, and we read together Isaiah 55:12: "Ye shall go out with joy, and be led forth with peace: the mountains and the hills shall break forth before you into singing, and all the trees of the field shall clap their hands." Guidance is easy when our will is His will. When we follow His leading, He promises we shall hear a voice behind us saying, "This is the way, walk ye in it" (Isa. 30:21). When we do that, even the trees will clap their hands.

7

Triple Ripple

The novelty was wearing off. Country life was a different style of living. The peace and tranquillity of those first happy days became a somewhat oppressive silence to my city-dweller ears. Here I was, stuck in my picturesque little lodge while all the action was happening a mile away at the youth center. I peered out my window through the bushes, rambling roses, and trees and contemplated my mission field! All I could see were the owls, cows, and black birds! Where were my fish?

"Start where you are with what you've got!" said the Master.

"But, Lord, haven't You forgotten something?" After all, I mused, with all He had on His mind it was perfectly conceivable that He had overlooked one or two details in my inconsequential make-up. He must have forgotten I was "good" with young people. This was obviously the area of my talent, and so He really must have made a mistake planting me among little old ladies in rose-bedecked cottages. I had no knowledge or experience of old age, nor did I wish to acquire such. This area of service could well be left until I, too, was seventy years old and lived in similar rose-bedecked quarters!

I was, of course, making the common mistake of telling God how I would serve Him and who I would reach for Him. I watched the little river bubbling over the rocks under the beautiful stone bridge near our house and threw pebbles moodily into the pool beneath me. As I watched the ripples, they seemed to echo the verse, "Ye shall be witnesses unto me both in Jerusalem, and in all Judea, and in Samaria, and unto the uttermost parts of the earth" (Acts 1:8). The Lord seemed to be saying to me, "Start where you are with what you've got (Jerusalem), the circle will widen (Judea), I'll lead you to people you don't particularly like to tell them of Me (Samaria), and unto the uttermost parts of the earth."

Reluctantly I gave in. Next day while wheeling our baby Peter in his pram and clutching the sticky hand of four-year-old David, I began my intrepid spy work. I felt like Caleb sneaking into the Promised Land. However, I found that my giants were hardly as imposing or frightening as his. I nodded cheerfully to little Mrs. T in her English garden, chatted to Mrs. S as she rocked on her porch, and at last plucked up courage to knock on a few doors and invite the ladies to my cottage to read the Bible. They were all very polite and said "Yes, thank you" they would be pleased to come.

I waited expectantly. It was a long wait because no one came. Disappointed, I tried to refrain from saying "I told you so!" to the Lord and returned to gently inquire of the ladies why they had not been able to come. They appeared embarrassed and offered varied excuses. I smiled cheerfully and reissued my invitations. They assured me they would be there next time. They weren't!

Well now, there was my responsibility over with. Surely I couldn't impose on their kindness any more! Shortly after these fruitless efforts on my behalf, a teenage boy who had recently come to Christ became concerned about his grandmother and invited me to attend the old age pensioners' meeting with him and his grandmother. I went grudgingly. I was still sure I knew far better than God how I should be used. I looked around the room. All the old ladies and gents were over sixtyfive years of age, this being the qualifying age to join this excellent group. They were sweet, but I was bored already. I must say, however, that I certainly was convicted by my young friend's obvious love and concern for these old people. The meeting began, and suddenly I was riveted to my seat.

"We will begin," said the chairman, "by reading out the death roll from last month," which he proceeded to do. As we all stood in remembrance of these souls who had gone forth into eternity, my young friend dug me in the ribs.

"See what I mean?" he hissed. "These people need Christ now!"

I was convinced and ashamed!

The next day found me knocking at doors for a third time. A few promised to come, and this time they kept their word. One was lame, one blind, and one deaf, and all were over sixty-five! The pebble dropped. Suddenly I found that I was surrounded by mothers and grandmothers, love and encouragement, wisdom and gentleness. I had no idea Jerusalem was so inundated with old people. We sang, we prayed, we read the Scriptures, and our numbers grew week by week. When the time came for our special Christmas meeting, we had to remove all our furniture and place it in the garage. Forty ladies gathered, and at the end of the service Stuart presented a homemade cake to the oldest lady present! He had all of the ladies stand up while we counted upwards from sixty-five. At last one little lady was left standing alone, beaming with pride. But she looked very surprised to receive the cake that Stuart happily handed to her. Then I told her she could sit *down*. There was no response. And someone informed me she wasn't the oldest at all. She was just stone deaf!

The ripples widened, the old folks' daughters began to attend the meetings, and we moved out of our little lodge into larger accommodations. I couldn't believe the love that was shed abroad in my heart by the Holy Spirit for this group of people. Starting where I was with what I had brought me a discovery of abilities that I had no idea I possessed. One day some of the mothers brought along their teen-age daughters, and my heart leaped for joy. The triple ripple! I understood the principle at last. What a perfectly natural sequence of events, and what a divine way to reach the young people — through grandmother praying and mother finding Christ.

"Now," said the Master, "we'll start and use all that talent you were boasting about!" Subdued, I wondered whether I was cut out for teen work after all. "You don't know your gifts unless you try to exercise them," said the Master. "Never decide where you should be used again. That's My business. Having started where you are with what you've got, let's just see where the ripple will lead you!"

8

The Barn

Women are always looking for some new interest or hobby. New pursuits are the spice of life to us. My Bible suggested a new one to me. I read in Romans 12:13 that I should be "given to hospitality." Apparently the word "given" meant to pursue. In Acts 16:14 Lydia opened her heart to Christ, and one verse later she was busy opening her home and pursuing Paul, Silas, and their friends to persuade them to stay with her. An open heart ought to mean an open home. I had let the Lord in when He knocked on the door of my life; why, then, did I find myself denying other people entry?

"Some teens are so easy to love, and others I don't even like!" I complained to the Lord.

"I loved you when there was nothing lovely to love!"

He rejoined. "While you were yet a sinner I died for you" (Romans 5:8, author's paraphrase).

"But don't I have a 'right' to invite whom I want into my own home?" I questioned.

"Your home?" my heavenly landlord inquired patiently. "Don't you remember you signed it over to Me, and isn't it lawful for Me to do what I will with My own?" We had been through all that before, so I hurriedly agreed.

"Since this is My house," He continued, "don't you think it is reasonable for Me to invite whom I will into it?" Next He pointed to my locked and shuttered heart that was so afraid of opening up and getting hurt and commented, "Remember, this is My heart too. Why don't you undo the locks and let Me in?"

"Oh Lord, You are in. Don't You remember I gave You free entry years ago!" (As if He suffered from amnesia!)

"As much as you do it unto the least of these my brethren, you do it unto me!" the owner of my property reminded me.

Just then the doorbell rang, and three members of our group who had been cycling by stopped in to see me.

There was a snake in my kitchen. He slithered around drawing my attention to many good reasons why this particular evening was not a convenient time to entertain: the pile of washing to be done, the half-finished letter to my husband, a baby's cry upstairs. I kicked at him (the snake, not the baby), missed him, but managed to tell him before he disappeared that I'd decided from now on to try and live a "plan-less" life like the Lord Jesus had lived. My schedule would from henceforth be set in heaven. I decided to stop minding God's business for Him. His was the responsibility; He could do the worrying!

"Come in," I said, grabbing the three youths and yanking them inside. "Oh, do come in. Thank you so much for coming!"

Rather surprised at the warmth of my welcome, they hesitantly entered my home and, though they didn't know it then, my heart. The harvest stands ready, but how hard are the hearts of the harvesters! The fear of the cost of involvement is so great, and often the heavenly farmer finds nowhere to stack His grain.

The harvest was truly ready in our small corner of the mission field. The laborers were few but fervent! Most nights of the week newly gathered sheaves began to be untidily piled around our house. Our little abode was used, but not abused. A small sign reading, "Where do you think you are going?" was usually enough to restrict movement from forbidden areas. We sang, we shared, we prayed, we opened the Bible and studied it verse by verse. We sought out the meaning, put it into our own words, and applied it to our lives and circumstances. It was piercingly relevant. Day after day, week after week the young people came, bringing their friends (and enemies) with them. From that time forward it was a question of committing the day to Him and accepting whatever happened as coming from Him.

There came a time, however, when "no more sheaves could be safely gathered in!" We were not in a position to "pull down our barns and build greater," and we prayed to the Lord for an answer to our predicament.

A young mother had been coming to the Bible study for many weeks. She was shy and sweet and needed a ride to the meetings. Each time I drove her home, I would pray, "Lord don't let me rush her into making a decision; help me to give her plenty of time to understand."

One day she said to me in exasperation, "Jill, when are you going to help me find Christ? I'd been praying ever since that very first study time that you would have the courage to speak to me!"

With my help, she ushered Christ in with her tears. The very next week her husband accepted the Lord, and together they invited us to use their "barn" for our meetings.

The sheaves were absolutely delighted! Two thousand years ago Christ had been born in a stable. It was obviously the sort of place He delighted to visit; and in the months ahead He was to be born again in many a teen-age heart. The premises were old and needed plenty of work. The temptation was to call a work party of worthy willing workers (adults preferably), roll up our sleeves, and do the work. Yet I felt it would be better to let the teens fix it up for themselves. We gave them responsibility (before they showed any), letting them splash paint merrily over everything in sight (it could always be mopped up when they had all gone happily home), and just made sure they knew it belonged to "them." The value of the united project was immense.

One elementary need, that of transportation, was wonderfully taken care of. A missionary, hearing of our lack of a vehicle, signed his mini-bus over to us. For years it flew busily mile after mile collecting and depositing excited teens. Sometimes it ran more on prayer than gas, but God always provided just enough money for our needs, though never enough to stop us from being dependent on the giver of our gifts. One day we had a blowout. Whether we couldn't afford to repair the tire or whether we simply forgot about it, I cannot recall. But I do know we never did replace that spare wheel. For years the bus served us well, covering hundreds of miles over rough roads, carrying gangs of young people to share their faith in Christ. The next blowout we had was the week after we traded in our old exhausted chariot for a new one. The new vehicle was, of course, accompanied by that saving spare wheel!

Leaders emerged as responsibility and authority were given to them. They were usually as surprised as we were by their accomplishments and began to spearhead new avenues of outreach.

"How would you like to captain a Christian football team?" we asked a fine boy who loved the Lord, football, and little boys — in that order!

"Oh, I couldn't do that!" he protested.

"How do you know if you have never tried?" we inquired.

Accepting the challenge, he soon had his team playing other local clubs. He would then invite the visitors back to the barn where the girls would feed them and a time of sharing would evolve. Junior teams sprang up, and boys between the ages of eight and twelve began to come around. We lovingly called this group "the beasties." If you have little boys between these ages, you'll know why we named them that! Individually they were great; collectively they were "the beasties."

God gave me a special helper and friend who had a patient and understanding love for this particular group. They drove everyone else to distraction, but Angela heeded our senior missionary's comment that "boys will be boys but one day will be men," and she gave herself unstintingly to the children.

Angela said, "If we can touch base with this gang now, even if it seems impossible to teach them spiritual realities at the moment, I believe we'll reach half of them by the time they're sixteen. If we wait 'till they're grown, we'll win only two or three of them!" She was to be proved absolutely right. We needed a vision. I learned that youth work needs to begin when the "youth" are five or six years old!

We discovered that children's Bible clubs could be set up on school premises. It necessitated lots of faith, much prayer, and a bold approach. For example: "Please, Mr. Principal, we have seven or eight teenagers who want to give their spare time to influence these little ones for God and teach them the Bible. This, of course, will make them better pupils and will also make you a mighty popular man among pleased parents! Will you help us?" Having said this, we took a deep breath, sent a telegram prayer, and tried to maintain a weak smile!

What relief and praise followed as Mr. Principal

smiled and said, "Certainly. Use what you will. It's a nice change to see teen-agers doing something worthwhile." Soon we had six clubs led by teens in different locations throughout the town. "Train up a child in the way he should go," says the Scripture. "And walk there yourself once in a while," added a shrewd thinker. Our teachers discovered that they needed to watch their behavior and attend to their lives. Leadership required a certain standard of behavior, a lot of growing up, plenty of discipline, and much study. What a wonderful way to keep teen-agers occupied — seeking to be like Christ and sharing His life with others. Many a time a boy or girl would come to us and say, "Since I've become a Christian I've had to stop going to the places I used to go to, so what do I do with all this free time I have on my hands?" Now we had opportunities of service for them, and we found out through this experience that entertaining newly converted teen-agers was *not* the way to keep them. "Employing" them was!

While all the children's work was developing, other teens were setting off to their old haunts to bring their friends to meet Jesus. "Operation Andrew" was soon in full swing. When they couldn't persuade their buddies to leave the tavern, coffee bar, discotheque, or dance hall, they began to call me and say, "Please come to us, Jill. They're asking questions we can't answer. They are interested but are afraid to come up to the barn." Immediately the snake flashed a picture in front of me. I saw myself slinking quietly into the entrance of the tavern while at the bus stop opposite stood the minister from my church and the local church gossip!

"What about your reputation?" he hissed. "What will people think?" (As if he cared anyway!)

I made an excuse to the boy on the telephone and hung up. Wrestling all evening with my pride, I busily wasted time. I knew I mustn't read the Bible. I'd be confronted with the answer! By bedtime, however, I was "willing to be made willing," which is the first step to

obedience! I opened the Book and was not a bit surprised to read, that He "made himself of no reputation"
(Phil. 2:7). The next night, head high, I walked into
the public house, sat down with the boys, and found
needy, interested souls ready to be reached. How was it
I had to learn the same things over and over again! It
was the triple ripple lesson — the widening impact, the
reaching out to the Samaritans. These were the despised
young people that many respectable "religious" folk at
Jerusalem wouldn't have anything to do with!

The success of the visit gave me an idea. If the young
people in this public house were as interested and open
as this, what about the myriad other pubs in the area?
"The best way to begin is to begin," said R. A. Torrey.
(There are some things you don't even need to pray
about! Remember?) Systematically we began to visit
each pub in our area. We sang, testified, or spoke for a
few minutes, then gave out Bibles and Christian liter-
ature and spent time chatting with the people. And
always we were invited back again. We were always
careful to ask permission from the manager. After explaining what was involved, we were never refused
entry. I felt this wasn't particularly a compliment to us,
as I could see that these men hadn't the slightest con-
ception of how Christ could change a man and fill his
life so completely that he would no longer need to be
drunk with wine. If they had realized this, I'm sure they
wouldn't have let us in to threaten their business!

Invariably as we entered a bar, something always happened which really sickened me. As we grouped around
their piano to sing spirituals or favorite hymns, the men's
hands would go into their pockets to fish out some
money. What a sad picture they had of Christ's glorious
church. Their actions said more clearly than words,
"Here comes the church begging as usual!"

Getting pretty upset, I would raise my voice and say
something like, "Folks, please, we don't want your
money. We haven't come to ask for something; we've

come to give you Someone. We are wealthy beyond
measure because we have Christ, and He is all we need!"
This usually got everyone's attention, and we were in
for a great evening of sharing.

It soon became apparent that we needed to get organized. Buying a map of the district, we spent one whole
evening spying out the land. We marked the pubs,
dance halls, coffee bars, discotheques, and open-air places
where young people congregated. Then we planned a
systematic blitz on each place in turn. One week it
would be street work, the next coffee bars, after that
pubs, and then the fairgrounds and amusement arcades.

We began to learn that different types of bait were
needed to catch different types of fish. Music was a great
attention-getter in some places; testimonies, skits or five-
minute sermons in others; and in some the need for
dramatic presentation became apparent. Therefore, we
wrote a musical play called *Sitting on the Fence*. It was
a simple story of a young girl sitting on a wooden fence
with the devil on one side and the preacher on the other.
The music and the story told of the fight for her soul.
We took this simple dramatization to open-air shopping
centers, coffee bars, and any other place that would have
us. It became a real weapon for the Lord, and is still
being used today in many parts of the world. I discovered that drama could be a real entrance into places that
wouldn't let us in "just to preach."

Many times we received a rough reception, but the
teens were simply exhilarated with the privilege of suffering for His sake! They were far more courageous
than I. Many a time I would be busy exhorting them in
prayer to be brave and to fight the foe — with bowed
head and knocking knees! When I opened my eyes, I
would find myself alone. The army was already engaged in the conflict, while I was still trying to get into
my armor!

On one such night after having launched the team
into their evangelistic work, I found myself without a

goal for the evening. I wandered toward a huge dance hall into which dozens of teens were streaming and out of which deafening beat music emanated. I began to pray. (Not very hard, in case He heard me and told me to be the answer to my own prayer!) "Oh Lord," I intoned, "give me the courage to go inside!" I neither expected it nor wanted it. When the courage didn't arrive, I heaved a sigh of relief and returned home to pray for the poor people in that den of iniquity. That night I "happened" to be reading in the book of Romans where Paul is being pretty logical in explaining the way the Gospel must be physically taken to the people who have never heard. "For whosoever shall call upon the name of the Lord shall be saved. How then shall they call on him in whom they have not believed? and how shall they believe in him of whom they have not heard? and how shall they hear without a preacher? and how shall they preach, except they be sent?" (Rom. 10:13-15).

"Well, I wasn't sent," I concluded. At once I remembered a sermon preached by my own husband on this very passage. Regarding this point he had said, "Some went and were never sent, some were sent and never went, some were sent and went!"

"I sent you," said the Lord. "You received your commission when I told you to go into all the world and preach the Gospel to every creature. That dance hall is the bit of the world to which I'm sending you."

The next week found me back at the scene of my defeat. I was disappointed when I discovered I felt just the same. Standing outside the dance hall all evening, I prayed. And this time I really meant it! But still the courage didn't come, and I retired home beaten again. Returning to the scene of the battle the following week, I began my usual demands for courage to do His will. Suddenly I realized something absolutely elementary. The courage might never come! Whether it did or not was totally irrelevant. I needed to obey. I needed to go in without the courage. It was a matter of my will and intellect motivating me to obedience. So often my obedience had depended upon my feelings. If I felt like it, I would obey. If I didn't I wouldn't! And so I applied my will to my feet (which I suddenly noticed had a snake wrapped firmly around them). "Feet, move!" I said. They did! The snake, who cannot wrap up the feet of obedience, hurriedly unwound from my ankles. I found myself inside the dance hall where the courage was waiting for me!

"Take me to the manager," a voice demanded. I looked around to see who had followed me inside. There was no one there. It was I who had demanded the interview! Once in the man's office, perfectly calm and collected, I heard myself asking if I might speak to the thousand teen-agers gyrating to the unbelievably loud rock music. After answering many questions and sharing Christ with the manager, an open door was set in front of me that no man could shut (Rev. 3:8). Surely God gave me favor in the man's sight.

Week after week young people found Christ in that place, and today they are in the vanguard of the youth work. And I learned one of the most valuable lessons of my Christian life: To obey, without stipulating conditions, is what being a soldier for Jesus Christ is all about!

9

Mary's Little Box

Days passed into months and months into years.
Stuart's ministry developed and took him away for in-
creasing amounts of time. Having once dealt with my
resentful heart about the issue of his absence, I didn't
expect to have to deal with it again. I learned the hard
way. Victory won yesterday does not mean victory
automatically dispensed for the rest of life.

Although I kept myself thoroughly involved and saw
much blessing, once more I began to fall prey to dis-
contentment and self-pity. I read the story of Mary's
little alabaster box of ointment. I believe Jewish girls
kept these treasured boxes of ointment as security. They
were their marriage boxes. If they never married, the
precious ointment would provide for them. If they did

marry, the proceeds would be part of their parental provision. They were, as the Bible says, "very precious."

So was mine! My marriage box again became more valuable than my relationship with my Lord and Savior Jesus Christ. I was amazed at how hypocritical I could be, pretending all was well yet knowing differently. I watched my senior missionaries and tried to copy their ways. I learned to wave my husband off on a three-month tour with just the right evangelical smile. With a false earnestness which apparently was believed, I mouthed the usual pious platitudes to those who sympathized over our separation. "Oh, the Lord will look after us. Don't worry. He will give us the peace we need and make it all up to us in some way," I assured them. Now this was true and I knew it, but I was frosting up solidly on the inside. The warmth of the Lord's provision was far from my experience. The problem was that I didn't want His help. I wanted my husband!

I stopped reading the Bible (it was far too relevant), and I stopped praying. After all, I had nothing to say and certainly didn't want to hear His voice any more. Why, the last time I'd turned to the Word for comfort, my eyes had been drawn to the words, "Is it not lawful for me to do what I will with mine own?"

"It may be 'lawful,'" I snapped, shutting my Bible, "but I think it is awful!"

At this point in my spiritual experience I hadn't learned that His rod and staff comfort the stupid wayward sheep. I didn't like the prods one little bit, nor did I appreciate His staff reaching down into my hole of depression to get me out. Depression suited me much better. The snake slithered in beside me, and we spent a few dreadful weeks hissing out our mistrust of God's ways.

"Don't give in," the snake advised. "If you do, you know He won't let Stuart stay at home; He'll just take him away all the more! Stand up for your rights! Let your husband know how unhappy you are. You know how to do that, don't you? When he says, 'Is anything wrong, dear?' say 'No, nothing' in such a way that he knows perfectly well there is!'"

I knew exactly what he was talking about and knew how well I could do just that. I was appalled as I realized the power I had as a Christian wife. I could so easily make my husband worry about me. I could hinder or even prevent him obeying God! Standing up for my rights couldn't mean that! The snake had overstepped himself again, and I suddenly recognized the source of my thoughts. I began to open up the lines of communication with God again.

"You don't know what it is like being so lonely, Lord," I accused Him.

"My Son left home for thirty years one time!" He replied.

"Well," I countered, "you don't know what it is like to be separated. You were with Him in spirit." The shadow of the cross and the voice of one crying, "My God, my God, why hast thou forsaken me?" was His answer.

"It was your sin, all that rebellion and self-pity and anger, that separated Me from My son, Jill. I punished Him instead of you because I love you, and it's because I love you that I want you to believe that! My will for your life is good and perfect and *acceptable*."

My disobedience had so numbed my feelings that my heart couldn't believe that His will could be acceptable. Endurable yes, but not acceptable! However, I could apply my mind and my will to respond. I must start reading the Bible again even though I knew I would read things that would convict and condemn me.

I began where I had left off — the story of Mary's little box. I fought a battle with my pride. I knew I should go and seek counsel from my senior missionary. She was one who had obviously yielded her marriage box years before and apparently was enjoying happiness and victory.

The snake's tail twitched in horror. "Just imagine her

face," he shrieked. "How can you bear to let her know you are a failure? Keep up appearances. Nobody needs to know your heart's condition!" I thought of Mary. How hard it must have been for her to bring her marriage box out in front of all those people and give it to Jesus. Everyone knew the disciples had left all to follow Him, and here she was with an unyielded box! What would they say? It would be much better to keep it hidden. She knew Jesus would never take it from her by force. Surely it was enough to sit at His feet, listen to His word, entertain Him in her home, and keep her little box hidden and intact.

At last I went and talked with my senior missionary. I discovered the breakage of her little alabaster box had been as difficult in her experience as mine. She was loving and sympathetic but very firm with me.

"Jill, you've given Him everything except this one little box; and it doesn't matter whether it's a marriage box or a box of another sort, holding back anything is backsliding. You'll never move one step forward, never hear His Word to your heart, never see an answer to a prayer, when there is known disobedience in your life!"

I thought again of Achan's sin in the Old Testament (Josh. 7:18-26). Buried deep within his tent was the treasure Achan thought no one knew about! But God knew. No depth of earth can hide the precious things we seek to conceal in disobedience. They only spoil, hidden within the cold earth. I, like Achan, knew my disobedience would bring trouble to my loved ones and to God's people. No more victories could be won until all had been exposed. How grateful I was that I didn't live in Old Testament times. If I had, I suppose I would have been stoned to death many times over by now!

I read Mark 14 over and over. "Lord, I can't give it to You. It's too precious. I'll never be like Mary; but if You will make me 'un-me-like' and work the miracle in my heart, I will give You permission to take it from me. I'm through struggling. I've had enough," I prayed. He changed my attitude, and the box was gone. The aroma of the ointment filled the house and the sweet fragrance of life attracted many people to the Savior.

But some disciples responded as they had in the Gospel story by telling me it was a waste. "God doesn't intend you to have a separated marriage! It could have been used some other way."

But I didn't listen. Wiping His feet with my tears, I spilled ointment and prayed, "Oh God, stop me from trying to scrape this up and put it back in the box again!"

"People will come to know about Me because of the aroma," God replied.

A miracle had happened in my heart. My situation was acceptable! I was at peace.

10

The Warehouse

"What we need now," an excited teen-ager commented, "is a big old warehouse!" I observed him with a certain measure of resentment.

"You need to learn to be content with such as you have!" I retorted.

"Typical teen-ager," the snake agreed. "They are never satisfied. You're quite right to be irritated. I think you're doing quite enough. Anyway, don't you think you need to consolidate?"

"Solidate" was what he meant. Set my feet in concrete was what he'd like! As far as the snake and his devices were concerned, all progress must be impeded at all cost! Late that evening, seeking to dismiss the teen-ager's bright-eyed excitement from my mind's eye,

I buried my head in the Bible. I read the exhortation in Luke 17:7-10 about the servant who had done those things which were simply his duty to do. I read that having done all, he was to consider himself an unprofitable servant. Well, I thought, that's a bit tough. It couldn't be referring to me. I thought proudly of all the bare harvest fields around. Surely He expected other farmers to do their share. It would be quite wrong to trespass on their property. Arriving at this smug decision, I was further irritated to be confronted again by the same waving young sheaf, demanding a warehouse to be stacked in!

"I found it," he shouted exuberantly. "A huge old warehouse. It used to store grain, and it's been empty for years and years. It's so big, four stories high, and it stretches a whole block. I've been through it too; there are old stone walls, wooden beams everywhere, crooked old chimneys and wobbly floors. There's a couple of dead rats in the basement and a bit of smelly water, but it won't take much to clear that up!"

That did it. The rats I mean! I appealed to the snake for help. He provided me with immediate, out-of-context Scriptures.

"Try 'Come ye yourselves apart and rest awhile,' " he suggested. "Or what about, 'So he giveth his beloved sleep'?"

"Just come down and look at it," the excited sheaf pleaded. "That's all I'm asking you to do."

And so I did, and one look was enough. The whole scene spelled "work" which I didn't like, "money" which we didn't have, and "time" which I wouldn't take. I promised the sheaf I'd pray about it, which was a great excuse for not getting involved.

A few days later an incident occurred which pointed to the glaring need for a new headquarters. I reluctantly turned to the "Word" for direction. I decided that if I found "anything" that directly referred to a warehouse then I would be willing to investigate the whole thing.

Of course my attitude was completely wrong. Unlike Gideon, who put his fleece out overnight knowing God could use the morning dew to show him the way, I decided to put mine out at midday when I was pretty certain there wouldn't be any dew around! I was going to search for my answer in a limited area of the Bible, thereby making it pretty hard for the Lord.

How foolish we mortals are. As if God cannot produce dew at midday if He wishes! Well, He produced a warehouse in the book of Malachi for me! Choosing in my ignorance an obscure portion of the Scriptures, presuming myself perfectly safe, I began to read. The snake, who apparently hadn't read Malachi either, curled up and went to sleep! I scanned chapter 1, relaxed in chapter 2, and let out a scream when I arrived at chapter 3, verse 10, which read, "Bring ye all the tithes into the storehouse . . . and prove me *now* herewith, saith the Lord of hosts, if I will not open you the windows of heaven, and pour you out a blessing, that there shall not be room enough to receive it!" The scream woke the snake and my baby. The snake was almost incoherent.

"I'm warning you," he screamed. "Snakes love warehouses, and if you dare buy I'll have one hanging from every beam!"

I told him to get lost. How could I ignore such an extraordinary verse of Scripture! I read the verse again, carefully and with a certain fearfulness, yet with a great new desire born within me by the Spirit of God to listen to His instructions and obey His Word! "Bring ye all," said the Lord. "That's the first thing. Prove me now; that's the next thing. Exercise faith to claim my promise that I'll open the windows of heaven, and there will not be room to receive the blessing." With the eyes of faith I saw in that moment a full warehouse. I heard the happy songs of the harvesters, saw the Lord of the harvest receiving honor and glory from the watchers, and I asked Him to forgive my fleshly reticence. I didn't have any idea how I was physically going to do more than I was doing, but I knew I had to try.

It's all very well to have visions in the night, to weep in acquiescing prayer, to claim the promises of God, but the time comes to get up and go! I had to become part of the answer to my prayer. So it was for Jonah. One day this bigoted, fervent Jew was praying to Jehovah. He was begging the Lord to do something with the aggressive Ninevites! God told him to go and be the answer to his own prayer. So he got up and ran – in the opposite direction! God brought him back by special submarine, and he then grudgingly began to preach the message God had given him. Starting on one side of the city, he preached his way straight through and walked out the other side. He then sat down to "watch" God work!

How often I was wont to do the same thing. This was all the wrong way around. God had sat down and rested after His work of creation was finished; Christ had sat down at His right hand after our redemption was accomplished; now "they" wanted to watch "me" work. It was my turn!

It would have been a simple matter to walk through the warehouse and out the other side, build my booth of observation, and sit down to watch the kids roll up their sleeves and get down to it. Jesus had chosen to show me a better way. The gospel narrative showed Him walking through the Ninevehs of this world preaching repentance. He had not passed through and then sat down in an observation booth in the heavenlies to watch God avenge Himself on our sin. He had lingered in the city to be the answer to our need. His were the hands that touched the dirty lepers. His were the hardened carpenter's muscles working for thirty years to provide for a widowed mother and her family. He hadn't walked past the cross to sit in judgment and watch us hang there seeking to atone for our sin! He had been crucified to become the answer to His own prayer for us!

Too often I hear people say they are not led of the

Spirit to do a certain job. Often this is nothing more than a pious platitude to cover our unsoiled, worthless hands. I knew in that moment of time that one day when I stood before my Lord He would gently take my hands and turn them over looking for the callouses!

The Lord had wonderfully arranged my home affairs to give me time for this venture. At the beginning of the work my little ones were in bed at 6:00 P.M., and I could be out at night when they retired, leaving them in the care of a baby-sitter. Now they were growing up and at school and I could be absent during the day. This way I was home when they were. What great opportunities now availed themselves to me to share Christ and give encouragement to the young people during many practical work parties. Working shoulder to shoulder with the teens, getting down in the unbelievable muck of a stagnant flooded cellar, and heaving bucket loads of slime up a rickety ladder brought a real sticky comradeship! It was activity not for the sake of activity, but with an object in view.

We certainly had our difficulties! One of my mistakes was made when we needed to lay a new concrete floor in the cellar. I had been advised to use a certain brand of concrete and promptly ordered one ton of "ready mix" to be delivered to the warehouse at 4:00 P.M. I instructed the man to deliver it onto the sidewalk outside the warehouse. Three times he asked me, "What exact time will you need it?" I wondered why he had this peculiar fixation about time; however, I repeated my instructions to dump it outside the entrance at 4:00 P.M. As I approached the building at 8:00 P.M. that night to prepare for the work party, I wondered where they had put the bags of concrete mix. I also wondered why I had never noticed that huge mountain on the sidewalk outside our building! It was then I realized that instead of receiving bags for "ready mix" concrete, I had received one ton of already mixed (and already set) concrete!

Frantically I rang the youth center for help. The men left the meeting immediately and ran to aid us with axes, picks, shovels, and buckets! They cut through the four-inch-thick crust, filled their buckets with the crumbly, heavy concrete, and, making a human chain, passed the whole ton down a rickety ladder into the cellar. About 11:00 P.M. I heard my husband's voice asking ominously, "Has anybody seen Jill?" No one had because I was hiding in a corner in the basement!

Despite my mistakes the warehouse was soon in use. It became obvious that God was busy instructing His angels to open His heavenly windows. I thought back to my promise verse, "Bring ye all the tithes into the storehouse," and wondered if I had fulfilled the conditions of blessings. "All" the tithes. Well, I'd surely brought in lots of physical hard work, but what about talent?

The snake and I had been reading the advertisements in the local newspaper. He had been suggesting that I go back to teaching to have some extra spending money. Not that extra spending money was wrong. It was just that the snake knew the Lord of the harvest house was planning on my fulfilling all the conditions, while he was trying to sidetrack me.

"Bring your trained talent into the warehouse, Jill," the Lord instructed me. "Start a nursery school; teach for Me."

"What a ridiculous idea," the snake protested. "What health authority would give you permission for a nursery school in this dirty place?"

I was inclined to agree, especially since I didn't particularly like the idea of working for nothing! The Lord took me back in memory to our daughter's beautiful dedication service. As I had held her in my arms, the preacher had given Stuart and me a text: "Take this child and nurse it for me and I will give thee thy wages." I thought of the hundreds of little children being offered to me with these same words.

"I will give you your wages, Jill; work for Me," said

the Lord.

So we buried the snake underneath the pile of news-paper advertisements and made a nursery school on the first floor of the building. The income from this venture finally provided wages for full-time staff for the youth work. The windows opened wider. We began to reach many families in the district. Each day in the nursery school we would have a half-hour of Bible study time and the children would take the things they had learned home to their parents. Soon the mothers and fathers came to us asking for children's Bibles so that they might help tell their children about God.

By now the work was expanding in all directions. Days hurried by—full, happy, hard-working days. Baby sheaves in the morning, big ones in the evening. The Bible is so full of promises to claim, I thought. I prayed, "Teach me, O Lord, that if the windows of heaven aren't open and my warehouse is empty, it's simply because I'm not fulfilling the conditions."

11

It's All Right for Abraham

Have you a besetting sin? Don't we all have one area of weakness in our lives that is weak forever? I thought about Moses. He had a fiery temper. He demonstrated it from his watery coffin by screaming in baby tantrums at the crocodiles. It manifested itself in cold-blooded fury when, after carefully "looking this way and that way," he murdered the Egyptian who was tormenting his Hebrew brother. He proved its dominion over him when he descended down the mountain having seen God face to face. Finding the naked, idolatrous worshipers, he lost his cool completely by literally breaking the Ten Commandments! Was it desperation or temper that caused him to sin by smiting the rock twice? Yes, it certainly appeared that Moses had a besetting sin.

The snake plays on our weaknesses. He is not a gentleman! He delights in kicking us when we are down and is neither sorry nor sympathetic. He hates us. He would destroy us if he could; and because he can't, he would render us desperate and inoperative by continually attacking our main area of weakness. Many times being aware of his devices doesn't even help. We can be fully aware of what he is doing; but after saying "no" for weeks, months, or even years, there can come a time when we say "yes." Perhaps we are lax in our relationship with God or lazy in our service. Maybe we are like David who was caught "looking" and forgot to bring "every thought" into captivity to Christ.

There came a time after the initial establishing of the warehouse that I found myself tired out physically and somewhat depressed. Metaphorically speaking, I was like David. At a time when kings should have been going forth to battle, I was staying home. As an old Chinese proverb says, "You can't stop the birds from flying over your head, but you can stop them from nesting in your hair!" That's true. The eggs were laid, and the young were hatched in my hair before I lifted a finger to do anything about it!

It happened at a meeting of all places. There I was, sitting on the front row in a packed room listening to my husband preaching a most powerful message on Abraham. Suddenly without any warning the snake, who was sitting beside me (I noticed his Bible was upside down), said, "Have you forgotten he's going away tomorrow for three months? You should be at home packing, comforting your poor children, and praying for yourself!" I tried to ignore him. After all, Stuart's voice was loud enough to drown him out. But he entangled himself around my Bible and tried to distract me. What was he doing? Well, he was actually preaching his own sermon from my husband's text! I couldn't believe that two such contrasting messages could come from the same source. As Stuart preached his heart out to hundreds of attentive teens, the snake was preaching one of his own messages right in my ear!

He was saying to me, "It's all right for Abraham. He was just like your husband. Look at him up there, all that faith oozing out. He's going off tomorrow to a land he 'knows not of' and will no doubt do great exploits for God. But what about Isaac? That's you!" As soon as I began to give my full attention to the snake's interpretation of the passage, I was in trouble. I shut off the preacher and turned on the snake! And I did it all "behind the smile"!

As I walked home I began voluntarily to wallow in a sea of self-pity. The snake was right. What about poor old Isaac? It was all right for Abraham, but it was Isaac who was bound upon the altar and would feel the knife! The same old struggle began; the snake was attacking the same old weak spot. The future, husbandless and lonely, stretched before me. My frustration grew. This had been yielded before. If the Bible said I was dead to sin, why was I leaping off the altar of sacrifice at this moment of time and feeling very much alive?

This was to be Stuart's last night at home before a journey that would take him to the primitive mission fields of the world. There he would help to minister to hundreds of missionaries who were tired and dry, having had no opportunity for spiritual food for months, perhaps even years. I thought about Isaac and how he had managed to acquiesce to God's plan for his life: He must have chosen to die. He was not a little boy, but in all probability a grown teen-ager. He must have submitted himself trustingly to his father's will, no matter how fearful he was. He must have believed they would both "come again" to the men who were waiting a little way off. In other words, he believed that life would come through death!

This was my choice. I had to get back on that altar and stay there. By the time Stuart returned, weary and ready to pack his bag and get to sleep, the battle was won. I handed my husband the poem I had written that clearly explained my inner struggle; then I printed the last verse in large letters at the front of my Bible.

An Isaac Experience

It's all right for Abraham;
God counts him as His friend.
Whilst I must be His enemy
Whose life He longs to end.
It's all right for Abraham,
Experienced in the art
Of glad obedience when it means
A dagger through my heart.

My father bound me hand and foot
And laid me on the pyre.
I wondered why God hated me
To torture me with fire.
I must be very wicked
Or have ceased to play my part;
I'd know in just a minute
When the knife plunged through my heart.

But greater than my fear of death,
My hurt at Abraham's aim;
His love for God transcended
The love for me he'd claimed.
Then God revealed the truth to me —
My *pride* had felt the knife;
That's why there was an altar,
The ropes, the fire — my life.

When you're bound upon the altar
By the hands of those you love,
You don't know there'll be deliverance
By the voice of God above.
Then *that's* the time to *trust the Man*
Whom God counts as His friend;
The faith of him who puts God first
Will save you in the end.

It's *not* all right for Abraham,
Young Isaac learned that day;
He watched his inward agony,
With groans he heard him pray.
And suddenly he longed to help
And cried in glad submission,
"Dear Father, sacrifice your son;
You have my full permission!"

It's all right for Isaac now —
It's all right to die.
'Cause if I die, I do believe
A resurrection I'll achieve.
I really feel quite lyrical;
I'm going to be a miracle!

I didn't know it then, but this was to be the last long
period of separation for us for awhile. I'm so glad I
made it back to the altar. My days were busy and
exciting, fuller than they had ever been. It was summer-
time, and open-air meetings were being held at a nearby
seaside town. A few churches in the town got together
and asked me to bring a team of young people to take
a service for them. They had set up the meeting in a
huge parking lot. At one end about 100 boys on their
motorbikes stood talking together. At the opposite end
the church people gathered, looking rather uncomfort-
able and slightly embarrassed. Between the two groups
there was literally a great gulf fixed! The microphone
stood exactly in the middle of the lot, and we bravely
began our meeting. We weren't getting anywhere, so
we quickly abandoned the microphone and the program,
approached the boys, and began to ask them questions
about their motorbikes. Eventually we began to talk
about Christ and found them as open and as ready to
listen as young people anywhere. We just had to be
willing to talk "to" them instead of "at" them. The
church folk gathered around, and we had a tremendous
time. One of the young people offered to buy us a cup

of coffee on the way home, so off we went to a huge motorway café that stood near by.

Suddenly one of the boys said to our girls' group, "Hey, we didn't give you a chance to sing to us. Why don't you have a go now?"

Before I could get out of my coffee cup to protest, the girls jumped up and began wandering around the café like wandering minstrels, pausing at different tables and singing their Christian songs. I hid behind a pillar of the building and hoped no one would notice that we were together! Soon the manager bore down on us, and to my surprised relief he informed me that he loved it! Would the young people come every week and sing! They would, and they did. The café held a thousand people and was always full in the summer months, especially during vacation periods. One day we asked the manager if we might use the café for a folk festival. He willingly agreed, charged us nothing for use of the facilities, and even suggested we charge fifty cents for entrance and give it to the missionaries! Thus began an outreach that regularly reached hundreds of people, some amazed travelers, and incidentally paid for three years' missionary training for one of the warehouse's greatest girls.

Why, I mused, is "dying" so much fun! The Bible says, "Except a corn of wheat fall into the ground and die, it abideth alone: but if it die, it bringeth forth much fruit" (John 12:24). I was learning that the way to up is down, the way to life is death.

12

Lovest Thou Me

"How would you like to be a pastor's wife?" my husband asked me. "A church in America has invited me to be their pastor." We had had such invitations before, but had never really seriously considered them. I had felt that Stuart's ministry belonged to the world. Why limit himself to one church and leave the wonderful worldwide opportunities he was being given?

For the next few weeks we received correspondence and phone calls from the leaders of this church, reaffirming their conviction that they believed it God's will that we should come.

"We're going to have to pray about it!" said Stuart cheerfully as he set off for another three-month preaching tour.

But how to pray? I found it difficult to pray from a
neutral position! By now Stuart and I were separated
for nine months of the year, and I had needed all my
prayers to give me the power to stop crawling off the
altar! With the possibility of more time together on the
horizon, it became difficult to pray "Thy will be done"
and mean it. Everything inside of me wanted so desperately for us to be together as a family.

Jesus had prostrated Himself before His Father in
Gethsemane and prayed thus, "If it be possible, let this
cup pass from me." Having been honest before His
Father, He had then used the "rope" of prayer to pull
Himself alongside the will of God, saying, "Nevertheless not my will but thine be done." I had to do the
same. Looking ahead at the prospect of being an evangelist's wife all my life, I was honest!

"Oh, Father," I prayed, "let this cup pass from me,
but nevertheless" — it took an awful long time getting
said, but there it was — "not my will but thine be done.
Please, Lord, give me the answer soon," I pleaded. "I
don't think I can stay willing for either way very long!"

There were more reasons for wanting to go than the
important personal need of a normal marriage situation.
For quite a while I had felt a sense of "completion"
where the youth work was concerned. It was as if my
work was finished and I had worked myself out of a
job. My co-worker had confided in me that she was
strangely burdened and called to involve herself full-
time in this ministry. She could easily assume the leadership if there was someone to take her place at mission
headquarters. And it just "happened" that there was!

The children were the biggest factor of all. I felt I
had failed in so many ways to be both father and mother
to them — especially to our oldest boy, David, who was
by now twelve years old. It was obvious he needed a
man around. Our little girl, Judy, was also beginning to
display signs of insecurity. I turned to the Word, fully
expecting to read something like Luke 18:28, 29: "Then

Peter said, Lo, we have left all, and followed thee. And he [Jesus] said unto them, Verily I say unto you, There is no man that hath left house, or parents, or brethren, or wife, or children, for the kingdom of God's sake, who shall not receive manifold more in this present time, and in the world to come life everlasting." I asked my Shepherd to lead us in right paths where His little lambs were concerned and sought special instructions.

Sitting on a beautiful English hillside beside a rushing, bubbling stream, I perused the gospel of John. Approaching the end of the book, I still didn't feel I had received any directive.

I pleaded, "Lord, help me to go on reading until I sense Your direction. You promised to show me the right path. Is it the right thing to do to put the children first this time? Please tell me." Continuing to read in John 21, I came to the question asked by the Lord, "Lovest thou me?" That was worth thinking about. Yes, I did love Him, even though my love was weak and poor. As Peter answered, so did I, "Lord, You know my heart. I am fond of You!" Then He asked me as He had asked Peter long ago, "Lovest thou me more?" More than what? Than Stuart, than my homeland, my children, and my people? More than these? I replied, "You know all things, Lord; I love You a little and I want to love You more. I would like to think I love You first." I think the Shepherd smiled. Anyway, He gave me my answer: "Keep your love for Me the most important thing in your life. 'Seek ye first the kingdom of God, and his righteousness; and all these things shall be added unto you' (Matt. 6:23). And now you will be shown the right path in 'this' instance."

"Feed my lambs." There was my answer! It was repeated twice for emphasis. "My lambs" He had said. I knew who He was talking about: David, Judith, and Peter. He was telling me they were His concern, and He had the very best in mind for them. He had planned for them in love. Seeing the birth of resentment in their

hearts before I had ever noticed it, He had moved to
make it possible for us to have the period of their growing teen-age years together!

Running down the hillside back to our home, I was
utterly convinced. After writing to my beloved mother
to tell her of the possibility of our leaving, I next put a
call through to Stuart in New York to tell him what the
Lord had been revealing. My husband had left home
feeling unconvinced about the wisdom of a move. But as
he sat in New York in a big convention meeting the
very night I called him, the preacher used a verse that
convinced him of God's guidance about our decision.
It was the same verse God had given me years before:
"One [of you will] chase a thousand, and two put ten
thousand to flight" (Deut. 32:30). We were going to
work together, and what was more we were going to
"live" together — how exciting and challenging! We
wired the church, accepting the call. Now all I had to
do was pack up and be ready to move.

"All" I had to do! I began selling everything. We
were to come to America with only our clothes. Everything else would be provided by the church, as this was
by far the most practical way to move a family 3,000
miles. After all, I thought, this would be a good opportunity for me to practice what I had been preaching. I
had often been quick to tell others that their treasure
must be in heaven, and we must never set our hearts on
"things," however lovely.

The snake sat on a packing case watching me. "All
those nice china wedding presents," he mused. "I bet
whoever gets them breaks them within a week!" All our
beautiful antiques sold for practically nothing! We had
been two short years in a cedar wood house that we had
built with our own hands. My mother had generously
furnished the home for us. It was beautiful and it was
ours, but now it had to go. I was sure I wouldn't get a
mansion nearly so nice in heaven! The snake added to
my despondency by telling me that he thought he had

seen one with my name on it up there that looked like a potting shed! I suddenly discovered that inanimate objects can come to mean far more than you realize. In a funny sort of way I was glad I had to prove I loved Him more than "these."

The next testing time came when our visa was delayed. Waiting, I found out, was one of the hardest things for me to do. Was it divine delay or the snake? It was hard to tell. Then I fell ill and had to spend time in the hospital. They gave me a scrupulous going over, testing everything I possessed (and everything I didn't know I possessed), until they found the trouble and sent me home rejoicing. If we had gone to the U.S.A. any earlier, I would have landed in the hospital on arrival. Divine delay it surely had been. Almost immediately the visa was granted, and we went to London to get it. As we paused before a statue of Abraham Lincoln outside the imposing American embassy, we began to quiz our children.

"Now then, the ambassador may ask you who is the president of the United States," Stuart began.

"Oh, that's easy," replied one of the children. "Dick Van Dyke of course!"

Seeing George Washington smiling down at their ignorance, I asked, "What's *he* famous for?"

After a long pause one of them stated hesitantly that he thought he had invented the telephone! Despite this rather disturbing display of ignorance concerning the land to which we were about to embark, we were received cordially, asked no embarrassing questions whatsoever, and traveled triumphantly home as the proud possessors of our immigrant visas.

The good-bys with our loved ones were hard, but the Lord provided a wonderful diversion at the last minute. Our beautiful golden retriever, Prince, was to accompany us to the U.S.A. Arriving late at the airport, we discovered the box we had ordered for him was far too small. We had "doped" Prince, and an argument ensued

over the slightly dizzy dog, while the children and I
boarded the plane. Relatives and friends watched in
fascination as Stuart and the officials argued out on the
runway. The people on the plane fumed at the delay!

"It's all because of our dog!" my daughter announced
proudly, while I disappeared under the airplane seat with
embarrassment!

Soon a larger box was obtained from somewhere, and
Stuart entered the plane and took a seat. Nothing happened. Another official approached my husband, and he
left the plane again. Apparently the box was too large
to fit into the hold. More delay. Then the door was shut,
and off we went minus daddy and dog! Looking down
at our waving relatives, we did not see Stuart. Then we
learned that the kind pilot had invited Stuart and Prince
into the cockpit!

When we arrived at London airport, a very drowsy
dog preceded my husband down the cockpit steps,
whereupon an elderly man behind me hissed, "Look at
that poor man. He's blind!" Another commented, "There
now, that's the way to deal with them hijackers!" We
giggled our way into the airport, eventually found a
new box, and praised the Lord for the amazing way He
had provided the amusing distraction for us.

We were on our way. We faced the challenge of a
new life in a new country. What would it be like? How
would the children adjust? Would I be a good pastor's
wife? I knew the Lord had led us thus far and that He
would be there to welcome us to our sphere of service.
I had proved that He was El Shaddai — the God who
was enough — and I knew from ten years' experience
that none of us needed more than an "enough" God.
Knowing that He would be there with all His adequacy
for the immense challenge ahead, I wondered if there
would be a snake in our parsonage?

13

Home Is
the Will of God

"Thank goodness, there won't be much culture shock," I somewhat naively commented to my husband. "We don't even need to learn the language."

"You don't?" inquired the snake with a snicker!

So, there was a snake in the parsonage. I might have known it! I noticed he had acquired an American accent that presumably would enable him to slink more unobtrusively around our new environment. In his nasty way, he was spying out the land hoping to cash in on my arrival adjustments.

No culture shock? The very first week I realized just how wrong I had been. Answering the phone, I listened to a friendly voice inviting me to a "shower." Completely baffled and a little embarrassed (the only "shower" I was accustomed to was over the bathtub), I hesitated. Mistaking my silence for shyness, the kind lady hastily added, "There will be about twenty of us there altogether!" This only confirmed my suspicions. I'd heard about strange goings on among American gals! More confusion lay ahead. "Where are the dust bins?" I asked a surprised garbage can collector! "Please put my groceries in the boot of the car," I instructed a shop boy. And later that day, seeking to quiet a noisy group of pre-teens who needed, in the American idiom, "to get it all together," I certainly achieved the desired results as I sharply told them to "pull their socks up."

Wandering through brightly lit, "huge" supermarkets among unrecognizable boxes searching for jam brands I'd never seen (jelly, I mean), learning our jelly was jello, corn flour was cornstarch, biscuits were cookies, and English muffins were a food I'd never seen in England, I began to feel as though I'd just gotten married and was learning the rudiments of homemaking all over again.

It was fun, though, until everyone started telling us how they loved our accents. Didn't they realize "they" had the accents? *Our* speech was English! Then, to add insult to injury, I was introduced at a banquet (only in fun, of course) as a speaker with an impediment in her speech! What a good experience it was for us to be foreigners in a strange land and see and hear ourselves as others saw and heard us.

The children adjusted rapidly. *Very!* Peter, our youngest, arrived home from school after his first week of American education, announcing triumphantly, "Oh mum, it's great! We don't have to say 'please' or 'thank you' any more!"

Judy had another problem. "*Who* are the nasty English redcoats?" she asked her father one day.

"Well, Judy," he replied, lifting her onto his knee, "there are two sides to every story, and this is the *wrong side!*"

Even the national holidays were different. And often embarrassing. "Mr. Briscoe," inquired a lady, "do you have a 4th of July in England?"

"No, madam," he replied. "We go straight from the 3rd to the 5th!"

But it was not hard to feel welcomed and relaxed. Everyone seemed so friendly and interested in us.

"Nosy, you mean," hissed the snake!

"No, friendly!" I insisted.

I encountered love and encouragement, warmth and hospitality, and beautiful generosity on every hand. One token of this was a lovely home, painted and decorated, furnished and equipped, all ready to settle into and enjoy. The modern appliances stood like silent servants ready to obey. Matching bathroom towels and soap made bathing a joy. Surely we could settle down quickly and get on with the work God had transported us 3,000 miles to accomplish.

Why was it, I dared to ask myself, that an irritating sensation permeated my mind? I sought to analyze it and decided I just didn't feel permanent. In fact, with all the reasons in the world to be content and at rest, I just didn't feel settled at all. What was home, I asked myself. Was home family? Surely home *was* family, and for the first time we had the privilege of being together. How grateful we were for this new experience. "Home" was a measure of security and comfort perhaps, and we certainly had this in abundance. "Home" was a house, and so I certainly should have been 100 percent at home in this beautiful abode. I felt guilty that my restlessness had to do with my not feeling at home in the house that had been provided, and I certainly suffered remorse for my unthankful attitude. Yet I *was* grateful. What was the answer to my problem?

Praying about my inner restlessness, I remembered Paul had prayed for the Ephesian Christians that Christ would settle down and feel at home in their lives. Was it possible that the Lord Jesus Christ could ever feel as

I felt within "my" heart. I thought of Him moving —
much further than the mere 3,000 miles we had traveled.
He had come from heaven's heights to the humble
temple of my life. Here was the secret, and God began
to show me the answer.

The inner rest and peace of heart could never be
found in any earthly mansion, however beautiful. A
heart "settling" experience of rest and security would be
mine only as I concentrated on settling Him down in
my life. It was not to be achieved through service for
Him, through speaking or teaching, or even through
enjoying our new ministry and family life together. Did
the holy Son of God feel at home in my heart? How
could I know? What did I have to do to satisfy my
heavenly guest?

One week later I discovered the answer. We had come
to the U.S.A. with ten suitcases. Everything else we
possessed had been sold or given away. One crate of
precious items had been sent by sea and took six weeks
to arrive. The crate contained a rather special English
rug, a copper kettle, the children's teddy bears or special
toys, and, of course, an English teapot and a package of
prized English tea!

When the postman arrived with that crate, he must
have thought we were crazy. Our excitement was ridiculous. We tore the big box apart, and each member of
the family carried his beloved items into their prepared
places. I heated the water, brewed my tea, and sat on our
rug feasting my eyes on the little copper kettle. It was
then that I recognized a deep inner conviction in my
heart. I felt at *home* at last!

Why? Well, these things were *mine*. They had come
from "home," and *that's* what made all the difference.
Suddenly I didn't feel as though I was on a permanent
vacation any more. This was it! I had arrived to stay.

My Lord spoke quietly to my happy heart. "It's the
same with Me. I entered your world without *one* suit-
case. No ministering spirit accompanied Me into the

darkness of Mary's womb. I grew up in Nazareth without a familiar heavenly thing around Me. All was strange to My divinity. Then I died and rose again to indwell the lives of all who would invite Me. You know — however beautiful, well-painted and decorated those human dwelling places are, I never feel settled in them until My heavenly furniture arrives. A chair of love, a table of joy, and all the 'good works' a wholly regenerated man should be thoroughly furnished with. As a man, as a woman, as a child settles *Me* down, I will settle *them* down because home is the will of God, and the will of God is to make Me at home."

So I took time to be still and concentrate on my relationship with Jesus. I sought to make sure He was comfortable in His home and asked Him to get the heavenly removal van going to furnish my life with His familiar things.

I felt pretty guilty about this little inner struggle and wondered if anyone had sensed my problem and interpreted my behavior as unthankfulness for this labor of love in providing our home. I was conscious of the importance of keeping our home as beautiful as possible. So many, many people made their way through the house, and all had an understandable curiosity to peek in each room. After all, so many had had a part in the time-consuming preparation. It was the *church's* house, not *ours!*

"Nosy interference," hissed the snake.

"No, understandable curiosity," I replied firmly.

Owing to a lack of church facilities, the senior Sunday school met in our house at 9:30 each week and occupied most of the rooms. Then we attended church service, after which I often served as many as fifteen for Sunday lunch. One Sunday evening we were to entertain some of our church leaders. So I marshaled the children and commanded them to assist me in clearing up the battlefield. "Just grab all the debris and stuff it into the big cupboard in the kitchen," I instructed them.

This being their sort of cleaning, they happily complied just in time for me to appear poised and serene to welcome our guests. I invited them to view the house while I brewed the tea. One dear lady assisted me in the kitchen. Just then the telephone rang, and I went to answer it. I watched aghast as she began opening drawer after drawer, cupboard after cupboard trying to find a kitchen implement. Clutching the phone and feeling quite ill, I actually watched the snake pulling her hand towards the overstuffed corner cupboard!! She opened it and was deluged with a shower of miscellaneous objects: wet tennis shoes, the dog's dishes, and the like. I turned red, white, and blue, which, while being patriotic, didn't help! The snake was nearly sick with mirth — laughter being a rare phenomenon to him. I noticed he stopped abruptly as he watched me preparing to be truly honest.

"Well," I said, carefully replacing the phone, "now you know what sort of a housewife I am!" Bless their hearts! Those ladies laughed and loved me just the same — even though my corner closet was so full of junk! I needn't have pretended to play the part. I had taken the first difficult step in learning an important lesson. I learned that as I was living in a goldfish-bowl situation, I wasn't to try being anything but the fish that I was! How foolish to pretend to be a cat or a dog! I had to learn to be myself and allow them to see I was human.

"Check around," the snake advised everyone. "If she wants to show you how human she is, I'll do all I can to help!" I didn't doubt that for one minute! After they had all gone home, the snake suggested to me that I'd really have to try a little harder. Being satisfied with showing my "humanness" wasn't good enough. "You'll have to impress them — live up to their expectations of you. Put on an act just a 'little bit,' " he wheedled.

The Lord Jesus contradicted him, laughed at my red face, and reminded me that hypocrite and actor come from the same root word. "My church is full of hypocrites," He commented. "Don't add to it! Pretending you are something other than what you are only makes a liar out of yourself," He pointed out. "Don't try and keep a corner closet in your life filled with junk. Give Me the run of your house, full permission to help you tidy up the mess, and don't try and stuff it away and hide it from *Me!* I'm here to help you pick up the house, not to pretend the mess doesn't exist. You must be prepared to be open and honest with your people as you are with Me; then they'll empathize. Then you can grow together without constantly living a lie."

How often we set ourselves up to be paragons of virtue. "I've given *all*," our lips say, while the corner closet, a silent testimony, stands full of hidden junk! "Oh, Lord, open it," I prayed.

14

Burying the Pastor's Wife

I noticed that at social gatherings I was introduced as "the pastor's wife." Each time it happened the snake snickered and pointed out that the other ladies present were not introduced as "the grocer's wife" or "the road-sweeper's wife" or "the garbage collector's spouse"!

"You're stuck with it," he hissed happily. "Every time you're given your title, a preconceived notion flashes across their minds. All of them will have varied ideas of just 'how' you ought to 'perform,' and as each will differ according to their church and cultural backgrounds, you will have to be a freak to keep them all happy!"

I thought about that. It was true. I, myself, had had my own preconceived notions of a lady with such a title. I had imagined a shadowy mouselike "personage

living in the parsonage," skulking about in the wings of a
dilapidated creaky house — hair firmly screwed into a
bun, her flat shoes facilitating the many errands of
mercy she must run. These "errands" were as vague in
my mind as the personage herself! What was she so tire-
lessly and piously busy doing? Succoring the dying,
mending other people's cast-off clothes for the poor
missionaries (only the best for God's front-line workers!), pressing the parson's Sunday suits all day Saturday,
and helping with the annual sale of work to pay for a
new church steeple to house more mice and bats?

"Help!" I gulped. "Please, Lord, not that!"

The snake was really enjoying himself by now. He'd
been working in his underground darkroom and had
produced not only a set of pictures of the pastor's wife
at "home," but also a set of pictures of the pastor's wife
at "work." These he proceeded to share with me.

"You must please the church," he intoned. "This is
your first duty." Of course, the snake doesn't care who
you please as long as you don't bring pleasure to the
heart of God. The church is an excellent substitute,
especially if you are "religious" and wouldn't be tempted
to please "the world." "They have a right to expect
certain things of you," he continued. "First of all, you
must play the piano!" At this he nearly swallowed his
horrid forked tongue in mirth!

"Well, that's *one* way I'd be certain *not* to please the
church," I commented, "unless they want all their hymns
played with one finger!"

Quite carried away, the snake continued. "A pastor's
wife must sit in the leadership chair at *every* women's
gathering. She must teach in the Sunday school (whether
or not she has an impediment in her speech) and must
never correct her children in public!"

I'd had enough. I decided the first funeral to be con-
ducted by me, *not* my husband, would be a final
ceremony when I would once and for all bury the

image of "the pastor's wife" under the life-giving soil of the Word of God.

What did God's Word say about the matter? I turned to 1 Corinthians 12 and found that the apostle Paul didn't want us to be ignorant about our spiritual gifts. I knew that the pastor's wife had the same responsibility towards God as every other church member — to discover her spiritual gift and to exercise it. But I also knew there were certain "duties" that went along with her privileged position for which she might not be gifted.

I didn't feel altogether ignorant as to my gifts. From past experience I knew that I had been blessed in starting things, exploding situations, moving into new areas in evangelistic outreach. I knew I had a gift of teaching and speaking and a gift of creative ideas for children and teens. But I was *not* a gifted administrator or committee member; I was not a good listener; and I could produce little "small talk" in company. Seeing that the latter gifts seemed to be the most obvious ones that would be required for my pastoral duties, I had considerable trepidation in my heart.

"Maybe these gifts would develop as I exercised them," I mused. Maybe I did possess them and just didn't know it. I thought back to the days at Capernwray Hall and the maxim God had taught me then. "The best way to begin is to begin." So I decided to begin and see!

But *where* should I begin? Should I just wait till someone asked me to do something? How did I get going? There were two extremely gifted ladies teaching the women's studies at church, so maybe the area of teenage activities would be a good place to start. There was no set meeting for them anyway. I began to work with a team of teens using our English musical drama *Sitting on the Fence*. Many adults helped me, and for the first time I enjoyed having adequate mature leadership.

But I did notice that Europeans and Americans had different ideas about leadership. It appeared to be a lot more "democratic" here than at home. I had been used to a "leader leading" and others following. The leader then constantly worked herself out of a job — not (I hasten to add) so she could recline on a spiritual bed of ease, but so she could lead off in another unexplored direction! I came to realize that I was leaving a lot of confused and hurt people in my wake, and after some painful situations I had to reassess my "scriptural" ideas of spiritual leadership. I began a personal study on the subject.

I discovered many things — the most important being that love is the answer. A leader *loves*. "Do you love only what you like?" inquired my heavenly leader. "Or do you love the unlovely?"

"I love only what I like," I answered honestly.

"Well, now," said the Lord, "you do have Me living within you, and I'm an expert at loving the unlovely or I wouldn't have stayed so long in the temple of your heart! The love of God is shed abroad by the Holy Spirit which is given to you. He will touch your hard, unloving heart and recreate a warm, loving one inside instead."

"How?" I inquired.

He answered with one word — "*Alone*."

"Alone?" I questioned. "What do You mean?"

I turned over the pages of my Bible exposing my mind, spirit, and soul to the Word. I read about the mourning Master depicted in the account in Matthew 14 when He learned of John the Baptist's death.

John and Jesus had run — had played — had romped through childhood together in Nazareth. John and Jesus had talked, had dreamed, had wept, had planned their days of ministry upon this needy planet.

John had gladly sent his dearest disciples to follow Jesus instead of ministering to him, and there upon the bank of his baptistry he had announced his Lord's presence. "Behold *Him*, not me. I'm not worthy to lick His boots! My cousin, yes, but more than human cousin — heaven's Lamb who taketh away the sin of the world."

"Baptize me, John!" commanded Christ.

"But I have need to be baptized of *Thee!*" John confessed. "Like all poor fallen humans (even though none greater than the Baptist had ever walked the earth according to Christ's testimony), I have need," he said. And so, cast into prison, kept by foul Herod, chained and beaten, the brave man continued to thrill the heart of God.

"Herod! You shall not have your brother Philip's wife," he thundered. And brother Philip's wife had had enough and planned a dinner party with the head of the prophet John as entree! Then came his disciples who took up the body, buried it, and went and told Jesus (which is always the best thing for us to do whenever we take up a dear human body and bury it). When Jesus heard of it, He departed into a desert place *alone* to weep for John's last torture, Elizabeth and Zacharias, and death!

How Jesus needed time alone. "My greatest transactions took place alone," my Lord told me. "Tell me, Jill, what's taken place lately alone with you?" There was a heavy silence. I had no answer. Not much, I thought! "It's alone I can touch you with the 'feelings' of other people's infirmities," my Lord continued. That really struck home to me. I'd always thought that verse in Hebrews said, "He was touched with people's infirmities," but it doesn't. It says, "He was touched with the 'feelings' of people's infirmities."

So often I had sung with emotion the words of the lovely song: "He touched me, oh, He touched me." But had He touched me? That *only* happens alone. Alone — grief is not allowed to sour into self-pity. Alone — He'll touch us and make us sad; touch us and make us cry; touch us with righteous indignation against wrongdoing; touch us with the "feelings" of others' troubles.

"Are there people you are trying to lead, Jill? Are there people you are trying to touch through the people you are trying to lead? Are there people near and dear to you in your own family circle whom you long to

have touched? Well, they won't be touched until you
are touched! If I can only have permission to get to
you, then I'll get to them!"

"But, Lord," I complained. "I've got enough infirmity
feelings of my own without collecting other people's."
It was then God challenged me with the multitude.

"Jill, the need of the multitude is as great today as it
was in this incident. Men, women, boys, girls — a multitude of need. They must be fed, taught, cared for, and,
above all, loved. When I was interrupted by the multitude that day, I had been truly *alone*. The result was
that I was moved with compassion. And that word
'moved' means convulsed! Are you convulsed with compassion for the multitude? If you're not, ask yourself
what has been happening alone."

I thought of my busy day. It had started with a hectic
morning, settling into a new country and a new house.
The phone rang continually: long-distance calls, short-
distance calls, calls of distress, and calls of mundane
detail. Our youngest arrived in the middle of my preparation to tell me a wild joke, while the older two
scrapped on the rug over something or nothing. The
dog had escaped early in the day, and now Peter came
to tell me our retriever had returned bringing with him
four people's doormats. I had a vision of stealthily re-
storing them at dusk. At this point our water pipes burst.
I looked at Peter and contemplated the multitude of
interruptions, and I was surely moved — but certainly
not with compassion.

"Peter!" I shook him. "My little multitude!" Looking at
me somewhat surprised, he retreated to Judy's room saying, "Hey, mummy just called me a little multitude!"

I knew my aloneness had been fake. Nothing had
happened between my Lord and me, or I, too, could
have faced my multitude of need with true understanding and compassion.

I thought about the miracle of multiplication in the
Bible story of the feeding of the 5,000. The "un-

touched" disciples had been commanded to feed the needs of the people. Having had a quick committee meeting and looked at the budget, they knew they were totally inadequate and had nothing whatsoever to give. Sure, they cared, but not enough. They didn't care like He cared.

"Give ye them to eat," He commanded.

"Send them away — let them get it from someone else," they replied. "We're bankrupt!"

The Bread of Life sadly stood by, grieved because they reckoned completely without Him. Their excuses were sensible, practical, thoughtful, and obvious.

"We're not bakers. We're fishermen. It's just not our gift to manufacture bread!"

"But I'm not asking you to make it," said Jesus. "Just to market it. I'll make it. You take it from Me and pass it around. Get near enough to Me so I can take you in My hands like those loaves and fishes. Let Me touch you, and when I do I'll bless you and break you and give you to the people. Then they will all be satisfied. They will know you love them. You touch Me; I'll touch you; you'll touch them." Leaders who will love must know what it is to be *alone*.

I thought of that little boy standing tall and straight, looking lovingly into the face of Jesus. "You're free to help yourself," He said. And He meant it! Not just my fish and loaves — my pitiful inadequacy in the face of multitudes of need — my heart, my feelings, my life, my all.

Jesus, I noticed, *took* it all! That's the only way to get the multitude fed.

"Can't I just keep *one* little loaf? That favorite one just for me?" I asked. "Can't I serve You without loving like You?" Before I asked, I knew the answer. I must let Him take all and touch me. He did. It hurt — but then it was that the miracle of multiplication began.

"Remember — the pastor's wife is a person (though she be married to the parson)," the Lord concluded.

"Find your gift and exercise it. Study the Word for the
principles and 'come ye apart' *alone* that I may touch
you that you may love."

"Please the church," screeched the snake.

"Please Me," commanded Jesus. "And then, give ye
them to eat!"

15

They're Leaving the Church

A dear pastor friend of ours had taken Stuart and me aside after learning we were about to take a pastorate and had whispered some words of wisdom in our ears. "In your new position, there will be a honeymoon period," he told us. "When the honeymoon is over, watch for a crisis to arise over even the most trivial of issues. People will then leave the church. Don't panic. And by the way — if you can possibly avoid it, *never* get into either a building program or a change in the church constitution!"

With his words ringing in our ears, we waited for the honeymoon to be over. The only problem was finding out just when it was finished because it never seemed to start! After being in the church just a few

short weeks, an important church officer resigned.
"He needs a vote of confidence, that's all," the church
leaders informed us. I felt it was we who needed the
vote of confidence!

"I'm afraid I don't feel confident about a man who
resigns almost as soon as the new pastor arrives," my
husband responded. "Accept his resignation!" The honeymoon sighed and tiptoed out of sight! The following
day we heard, "They're leaving the church." We came
to realize this little phrase was the title of one of the
snake's "top 10" records. He plays it in countless pas-
tors' ears. The words of the song come to the pastor's
family in whispered tones, passed on from one voice to
another or in unison as a congregation.

Immediately you have a vision of a packed pew with
a yawning gap in the center which draws the immediate
attention of everyone in the service. The pastor is then
put in the position of not knowing what to do. Is the
rumor true? Does he get a chance to talk the issue over,
or is he suddenly confronted with empty spaces before
he fully realizes what is happening? And if he is well-
informed from a reliable and unbiased source, does he
then heroically cast himself in front of the metaphorical
church door saying "over my dead body"?

Well, we soon learned that to run after everyone
who was rumored to be "leaving the church" meant
acquiring a spiritual olympic running record. As the
pastor's wife, I was definitely against running. It was
much easier to face the empty spaces than the angry
faces! Also, the snake had the most irritating habit of
standing at my elbow as the offended person approached
while he put the most snakelike ideas into my head.
Like, "When you shake hands, crush her fingers!" Or,
"Kick her in the shins." It was hard for me to cope with
the people who decided to stay and make their grievances
known.

To my surprise, my husband cooly encouraged anyone who wished to leave to do so. "Both doors of our

church are open. The front and the back!" became his
motto. I decided to stand at the front door to shake
hands in the future!

The snake had immediately noticed my overreaction
to criticism of my husband. He knew it was a far harder
thing for me to take than criticism of myself. He
planned to use this to his advantage, and it wasn't long
before he had an opportunity to do so.

Within a year of our arrival at the church we found
ourselves in the middle of a major issue: a change in the
church constitution! Sitting in a pretty highly charged,
emotional church meeting, I realized how deeply people
were feeling. There was much discussion over a doc-
trinal point that to me was a secondary issue, having
nothing to do with salvation. I watched people literally
"leaving the church" from that gathering, and I was
completely floored by the whole thing. The snake saw
his chance and took it.

"It's a shame," he hissed sympathetically. "Why don't
they ask their spiritual leader's advice. Why won't they
respect his great biblical knowledge? Get up on your
feet and stand up for your husband. He needs you to
help him out of this hole!"

Now, one thing my husband didn't need at that
moment of time was intervention. But up I got, managed two sentences, then burst into tears!

"Poor thing," smirked the snake, handing me a copy
of the church constitution with which to blow my nose.
"Try again!"

I managed to ignore him and retreat to the ladies'
room where I had some prayer with a dear Christian
friend. When I returned red-eyed to the scene of my
disaster, the church was in prayer. The crisis was over
— the people had left — and I had begun to learn some
new and necessary lessons.

First, after prayer and guidance we must do what we
really believe the Lord is leading us to do. We only
wanted the best for His work in this place. At the same

time, we had to respect other people's views and feelings and in no way allow their departure from our fellowship to make any difference in our attitudes and relationships with them. Now that was the hard thing.

I remembered the rebellion of King David's son Absalom and his eventual downfall. I thought about the edict permitting him to dwell in the king's city for three long years yet never being allowed to see the king's face. Can you tell me King David knew no sorrow? Of course, he did. So did a repentant Absalom. Deep anguish and confusion of heart accompany any schism in "the family."

I learned to *face* people after violent confrontation. This is an extremely important thing to do. To be mature enough to agree to differ or to agree to disagree without being disagreeable is a miracle only the Spirit of grace can accomplish.

The test came the first time I encountered a person who had left our fellowship. It was in the supermarket. There she was buying bread, and I had an almost irresistible desire to bury myself in the green vegetables and try to look like a lettuce until she passed by! The Lord helped me approach her and happily inquire if she had found a church home where their needs were being well-met. I suddenly realized that she was more embarrassed than I and seemed genuinely pleased I'd made a move towards her. We chatted, and she told me they were well-settled into a good church fellowship with which they could more happily identify, and I told her quite sincerely how glad I was it had all worked out well. We have remained good friends.

I learned that I *must* take the initiative if and when the opportunity occurs. But I also learned to pray and wait for the opportunities. Often I needed to grow in my attitude or knowledge of the situation. In our human families some members have to grow up a little before harmony is achieved, and the Spirit often cautions us to "wait" if one party isn't quite ready to cope with a fence-mending operation.

Humility was the key. The humility of each esteeming the other better than himself (Phil. 2:3). And also a practical determination to be cheerfully friendly whenever an encounter occurred "after" the event.

The main temptation I had to combat was to refrain from a telephone campaign. My womanly reaction to criticism of my husband or myself was one of immediate self-justification, self-righteousness, and a determination to vindicate us in the eyes of a friend. No one likes stones thrown at them.

"But one can always pick them up and throw them back," the snake interposed. "Retaliation is scriptural," he continued. "Jesus took a whip and threw the money changers out of the temple — remember?" I thought about that. The snake, of course, was misquoting Scripture again, so I knew I needed to look at the context.

Jesus never retaliated on His own behalf — only on the behalf of His heavenly Father or on behalf of the poor and oppressed. These people who were leaving our church were people the Lord Jesus had died for and loved as much as He loved me. Sometimes I found that hard to accept! If we are honest, we have to admit that we don't really believe God could love *anyone* as much as He loves us! But He does. What's more, even if they are doing something that grieves God, are we any better? Are we always right in thought, word, and deed?

How easy to be like the self-righteous Pharisees who took the woman and placed her in the midst of their enlisted mob of sympathizers and picked up stones of condemnation to hurl at her. It happened in the temple — even in the presence of the Lord Jesus Himself.

My Lord took me to John 8:1-11 and spoke to my heart concerning such verbal stone-throwing. "Put your stones down, Jill. Unless of course you are without sin. Judge not lest ye be judged."

"They're leaving the church." We would hear it

many times. And each time we would have to search
our hearts to seek His mind and follow His leading. We
must respect the other person and his important point of
view. We are responsible only for our attitude, not for
the attitude of others. And we are *never*, no never, to
pick up stones!

I caught her in the act!
She *lied* to me.
I rushed her to my friends. They shouted *"Guilty!"*
I stooped down to the ground to pick up stones
        of condemnation,
Then saw the writing in the dust — my Savior's
        proclamation:
    Without sin? Throw!
    With sin? Go!
    Before I cast My stones at thee.
    I've caught you in that act —
    You've lied to *Me!*
And in the courts of heaven they shouted *"Guilty!"*

I caught him in the act.
Adultery.
I told the gaping crowd. They sneered and sniggered.
I stooped down to the ground to pick up stones
        of accusation,
But saw the writing in the dust — my Savior's
        proclamation:
    Have you been true?
    Heart and mind through?
    The thought is worthy of the act.
    You stand unfaithful too,
        To him and Me.
And from the courts of heaven echoed *"Guilty!"*

He caught me in the act of all that's sinful
And ushered me to the spires of heaven.
The angels stooped to pick up stones of righteous
    indignation,
Then saw the blood drops in the dust that spelled
    justification:
Go — sin no more.
These stones you store
Within your heart leave here with Me.
Judge not, lest ye be judged.
And in the courts of heaven they shouted "*Glory!*"

16

Retreat to Advance

We were settling in well, I thought. The children were happy. The work was expanding, and I hadn't made too many unforgivable blunders. I was enjoying working with the teens on our musical drama. It was a challenge, and teens were obviously my niche. Then it happened! A knock on the door, a charming lady, and a warm invitation to come to her home, meet her neighbors, and tell them about Christ.

Well, there didn't seem to be any harm in that. One little meeting would be all right, even if the lady didn't belong to our church. She visited regularly enough, and if her friends wanted some questions answered, I would be happy to oblige.

Arriving at the lady's beautiful home, I discovered a

room comfortably full of talented and intelligent ladies.
I gave my testimony, got up to leave, and was asked to
return to teach the Bible.

"What do you want me to teach you?" I inquired.

"Answer our questions."

"What questions?"

"Why does God allow suffering? Why do some people still believe in hell? Why is the Old Testament still
read today when it's obviously out of date? How do you
find God? What is a Christian?"

I couldn't believe they wouldn't know the scriptural
answers to these things. But apparently they didn't or
they wouldn't be asking! Surely it wouldn't do any
harm to take a few weeks and do a basic doctrine study
with them. I suggested working through my husband's
basic Bible study on Christian doctrine entitled "Discovering God." They were so sweet and enthusiastic,
and the next class saw more ladies than ever. By the
end of six weeks approximately sixty of them were
meeting regularly.

The snake slithered happily home with me one day
and hissed, "Now you're in for it. Don't you realize
what you've done? There's not *one* lady from *your*
church there. These ladies all belong to another church,
and what's more, you are teaching them things their
minister may not like. How dare you sneak in among
his flock subverting his sheep! And then there are your
own church ladies. Wait until they hear about all that
you are doing. I'll make sure I put all the right ideas in
their minds about your motives. I'll make them jealous
and sow seeds of misunderstanding all over the place."
He ran out of words. His horrid little eyes were glisten-
ing as he visualized the damage. I didn't doubt his ability
for one moment!

As I thought about it all, one of our own women's
Bible teachers resigned because of ill health, and I was
asked to take over! My immediate reaction was to drop
my class and do so. My husband, as usual cooler and

calmer than I, sounded a note of caution. He knew it
was taking me hours of study to keep ahead of my enthusiastic students, and he wanted his shirts washed!
There was no way I could prepare two lessons a week
and cope with the youth work as well, even if he gave
up wearing shirts completely! He suggested I continue
the study but take it out of the homes into a neutral
meeting place. This way our ladies could come and the
teaching work that had begun could continue. After all,
we could hardly bring sixty ladies from other churches
into Elmbrook!

"But what will 'they' say?" I asked.

"If it's of the Lord, He will put His seal upon it,"
Stuart said.

"But what a start to my relationship with our church
ladies," I argued.

"You didn't seek this. You just took an opportunity.
Now follow His leading," was his reply.

The snake was furious. I don't know how much of
the future he knows, but he obviously knew enough to
see the blessing ahead. He was at my side constantly,
making sure he passed on all the discouraging comments
he heard around church. I knew some of our ladies dis-
approved, and I so desperately wanted them to be part
of it all.

We took the meeting into the basement of a bank,
and the attendance grew to over 100 ladies. Next, we
rented a theater in a local shopping center, and after
two years' ministry rejoiced to find 400 ladies coming
week after week to study the Word of God. Our church
ladies were great and eventually became the backbone of
our interdenominational committee.

The snake hated the theater. He much preferred a
little meeting room somewhere with a lot of overfed
Christians being stuffed yet stuffier! He hated the hunger
and the interest and the renewal of so many lovely
women. He hated the way some were born again, mar-
riages healed, and prayers answered. He hated it all. I

didn't underestimate him. I knew he wouldn't just sulk in the back seat of the theater. We are told not to be ignorant of his devices. We need to watch and pray!

Finishing our series of Bible studies in May, we decided to join together with two other Bible teachers from our church and have a one-day retreat. We had no idea what was in store. We managed to obtain the use of a lovely Roman Catholic college and gave our studies a name for the day — "The Liberated Woman." It received widespread press interest and even TV and radio coverage. We watched as 900 ladies signed up.

We stumble by surprise on so many of God's great purposes! He wanted the city won for Him while we were far too partial in our outlook. What next? We decided we would have more Bible study and then a combined two days of retreat. That was a step of faith in itself to have a retreat in January in snowy Wisconsin! It kept the girls on their knees, that was for sure. The two days were to be identical programs. This time we rented a huge new exposition center and managed to keep the price down to $3.00 a person. The program ran from 8:30 A.M. to 3:00 P.M. combining lectures, small group discussions, prayer time, music and testimonies, fellowship and sharing. The Lord gave us 2,100 women over the two days.

"Where do we go from here, Lord?" we asked. The question in our minds was, "Do we just get bigger and bigger or should we grow by spreading the time over more days instead?" The program appeared to need variation. "We'll try a weekend first and then a whole week of women's convention next year — how about that?" I suggested. The gallant committtee answered, "Let's go," so we set off to plan and pray.

Meanwhile, wonderful doors of opportunity were opening up for me — speaking engagements that would take me all over the country. Up until now Stuart had been the traveler and I had stayed at home. Now it was to be a little different. The snake saw his opportunity and took it, of course.

17

Have Bible Will Travel

The snake fastened his seat belt carefully and settled back for take-off. He pointed out how the windows rattled and the floor shook. And how the right wing didn't look too safe to him at all. "Have you noticed how the wings vibrate?" he inquired of me earnestly. I turned pale. All that flapping about seemed a bit dangerous to me. Surely it would weaken the joints!

"Why don't you move into the aisle seat," he suggested next. "It might balance things up a bit. Haven't you noticed how everyone is sitting along one side?"

Now, this was getting quite ridiculous! Here I was a complete bag of nerves. I hated flying. My heart was thumping, and I felt quite sick with fright every time there was a bump. I tried to be logical and remember my husband's reassurance on a previous trip. "You won't go to heaven one moment before you're meant to!" I just thought the moment I was "meant to go" had arrived. I got out my Bible and notes and started reading to take my mind off the journey. The subject I had been asked to teach was — *"faith"*! One little five-letter word — *faith*! Trust? Dependence? How could I possibly speak on that when I was reduced to a shivering heap of jelly by an airplane trip?

"Lord," I prayed, "You're going to have to give me victory before I get off this plane or I will have nothing whatsoever to share with these ladies!" And He did. One little phrase from my husband's' message that Sunday returned to me. He had made the statement: "The initial avenue of spiritual experience is the mind." Then the Lord brought one verse of Scripture to remembrance. "I will trust and not be afraid." My mind told me the object of my faith was trustworthy. I got my intellectual feet on that rock — then I applied my will. "I will trust. I will not be afraid, starting from now," I announced loudly in the snake's ear. He hastily disappeared into the seat pocket. The emotions followed — *peace.* I can honestly testify that God dealt with my fear of flying that day. Praise Him! It was also helpful to share that experience with the ladies during my talk on "Faith" the first evening of the conference.

At my first big ladies' meeting, I had an unnerving experience. Feeling decidedly unsure of myself, I wandered into the reception area. No one recognized "the guest speaker," of course. So I stood there looking hopeless and helpless. All sorts of panicky feelings began to take over. The first session alleviated some of them, and I began to relax. As soon as the counseling was over, a lady approached me and invited me to her room. She then announced that she wanted to cast the demon out of me! I looked at her and my mouth fell open! I felt quite hysterical for a moment and then was able to assure her that I didn't have a demon and asked her

where she had been hearing about demons. She appeared
to be extremely confused. The way the Lord gave me
Scriptures to counsel her was a real encouragement to
my own soul. Over and over again at these conferences
I was to meet all sorts of ladies with many, many "ex-
treme" theological ideas. I became more and more convinced that a balanced knowledge of the Word was the
answer. I studied my Bible as I'd never studied before.
I had to know the answers to the questions before the
questions ever came. I must be balanced myself. I needed
to learn the whole counsel of God. I realized an over-
emphasis on any doctrine of Scripture is a potential breed-
ing ground for a heresy, and I had to do my homework.

I began to enjoy the weekend conferences. I was determined to push away the snake's photo displays of
confusion at home: the vision of Judy falling off her
bike, or David and Peter having fights no one refereed,
or Stuart not being able to find either of his preaching
suits because I'd forgotten to pick them up from the
cleaners! Once I'd been away a few times and had not
been met by weeping deprived children, I realized things
were fine.

Relaxed, I could now benefit from the fine teaching
of my fellow speakers. Enriched and challenged by new
ideas and methods of evangelism, I could return home
to share these relevant ideas with our own ladies. I felt so
privileged to get to know many of God's special people.
However, I was often overcome with a sense of the
ridiculous. Usually it happened just before I had to get
up and speak.

The snake would whisper in my ear, "Who are *you*,
anyway? What Bible training have you had? What are
your qualifications for speaking with such great authority
from the depths of your ignorance?" Then the Lord's
quiet assurance would come. "Her qualifications are My
commission to go and make disciples and her enabling
is the Holy Spirit. Who shall lay anything to the charge
of God's elect? It is God that justifieth. Who is he that

condemneth?" It was then I remembered that one of the snake's names is the "accuser of the brethren." The snake wasn't the only accuser of the brethren, or rather the sistern! Others took a similar line.

" 'I suffer not a woman to speak!' How can you expect God to bless you when you flagrantly disobey His Word?"

The snake was quick to follow up the advantage. "Don't you remember the time you were speaking to the students at Capernwray Hall about youth work and those four upstanding new converts, all men, left the lecture hall because a woman was teaching? They knew you shouldn't be doing it!"

I remembered all right. That had hurt! How did they think I could speak with such peace and joy in my heart if I was sinning?

I knew different denominations held different views about lady speakers. They varied considerably. I, myself, disliked most women speakers. I'd rather listen to a man on most occasions. But what *did* the Word say? It appeared to be a relevant subject that needed looking into, since I was receiving numerous invitations not only to address teens and ladies, but mixed groups as well.

Now, this was not a new problem to me. Almost as soon as I became a Christian I heard totally opposing views about the matter. One group I met with refused to let ladies even pray aloud in a mixed group, and yet this same church allowed their missionary women to preach, teach, and pray out in "darkest Africa." That didn't appear to be very consistent, and it also gave me the feeling that God liked using men instead of women who were obviously second-rate material! I knew this was not scriptural, as the Bible plainly states in Christ there is neither male nor female — all are one in Christ Jesus. Then again, ladies were forbidden to speak to a "group" of men but were expected to witness on a one-to-one basis! What difference did the plurality make, I wondered.

Paul obviously listened to Phillip's daughters, all four of whom were busy exercising their speaking gifts. There was no rebuke recorded in the Scriptures from Paul on the occasion of his visit with them. The context of the relevant verses in the Scriptures had to be considered too against the culture of the times.

The big scriptural prohibition appeared to be the principle of usurping the authority of the man. If, therefore, the men of a fellowship in whom the care and oversight of the flock had been entrusted invited me to exercise my spiritual gift among them, I could know I would not be usurping their authority. If, on the other hand, I marched into an assembly uninvited and stood to preach, I would certainly be out of order.

I believe whenever men of God recognize the gifts of God in women of God and encourage them, under their leadership and guidance, to exercise these gifts, the work of God is expanded.

I was not prepared for the next attack of the snake. It was pretty subtle. I was to share the podium at a large meeting with another speaker I had never met or worked with before. The moment I was introduced to her I found myself instantly reacting, and I was not honest enough to call my reaction what it was.

The snake who has rare flashes of honesty (only, of course, when it suits his purposes) faced me with the truth. "You don't like her. You don't even want to sit and listen to her speak. And how can you possibly take the meeting tomorrow with that attitude?"

While the lady was speaking, I began to read the Word asking the Lord for a direct rebuke. I got one! Coming to Matthew 12:48 I read Jesus words. "Who is my mother? And who are my brethren? . . . Whosoever shall do the will of my Father." Well now, this dear lady was *family*. She was my sister! She was busy doing the will of God. As in earthly families, I realized I would be closer to some sisters than others, but the bond was there. I asked the Lord for the right sisterly feelings and immediately received a warm appreciation for the woman. Thereafter we had a great time together. God's forever family is forever, so I guess the closer we get acquainted down here the more we shall enjoy each other up there!

Another temptation I found I needed to combat regarded the subject matter I was to present. So many of my co-speakers had such wonderfully dramatic testimonies.

"Maybe you could color yours up a bit," the snake helpfully suggested. "After all, you are 3,000 miles away from home and nobody will know!"

Exaggeration has always been a problem with me. Too often I indulgently call it my wild imagination — instead of lies! The snake continued taunting me with the fact that dry Bible stuff wouldn't hold their attention after listening to someone relating how she had murdered her mother with an ax! I would find myself looking over my notes again and again. Maybe I should tell more stories. Maybe I could dramatize it more. Was the straight exposition of the Word of God sufficient to hold people's interest? Back from its precious pages I received my answer: "My Word shall not return to me void. My Word is a light and a lamp for people who are frightened of their personal darkness. My Word is like a fire burning up the dross of people's lives and like a hammer demolishing the rock resistance of hardened attitudes. My Word is a seed growing in the garbage dumps of wasted territory, producing flowers and fragrance instead of weeds and thorns."

I was to preach the Word, not my experience! Here and there illustrations from my experience would help to explain the Word, but I learned my lesson well. He promised to bless the promises of His Word, not the preaching of my experiences!

Time and time again I watched the power of the Word produce not emotion, but conviction. There was a difference.

Near my home in England there was a little English

graveyard. In the ancient plot lay an extraordinary grave. The old stone had been split asunder, and through the middle of it rose a huge oak tree, its branches lifted toward the sun. Sometime in the past, one little acorn buried in the earth beneath that stone, possessing the fantastic dynamic of life, had found the incredible power to split the stone wide open. It was the *Word* that had accomplished that very same thing in my life. The dynamic of life in the seed of the Word of God. It had been the truths of the Bible that had brought life from death in my own personal graveyard.

Almost at once the Lord taught me to pray for "conviction" of sin that would last, not emotion that would soon be past. Conviction is the Holy Spirit's business. He will convict the world of sin, of righteousness and judgment. The Bible teaches that this conviction usually manifests itself as an emotional low, not an emotional high, and is absolutely necessary before God's promises can bring release and peace of mind. What could I give these ladies that would hold them fast a few weeks away from the experience of a retreat? Doctrine, teaching, facts: the *Word*. In temptation, they would need the *Word*. In witness, they would need the statement of the *Word*. This I would give and refuse the temptation to paint an untrue picture of a wildly depraved life with all the accompanying gory details.

A new motto was born: Have Bible — will travel. Have Word — will tell. Have Peace — will triumph! "Go ye and make disciples," he said. And so I did!

18

The Wine Tasting

Elijah had had a good morning in church. The whole of Israel had turned out for the service, and it was a pretty fiery sermon. Literally! God had demonstrated His power in a supernatural way, and Elijah had finished off the prophets of Baal in a gory after-meeting. Facing Ahab, weak "King Compromise," Elijah told him to get back to his chariot and head home because the rains were coming.

Now the sky had never been bluer, the sun never hotter, the sand never dustier, but Elijah possessed the ears of faith. He heard the sound of abundance of rain. Up his mountain he went to pray — fervently. I believe he still would have been up there today if the showers of blessing hadn't come. His servant would still be run-

ning back and forth looking, watching, scanning the
horizon for the rain cloud with old Elijah exhorting him
to *watch* and *pray*! And it came, for the effectual
"stretched out" prayer of a righteous man availeth much!

What a picture of triumph! Followed so soon by defeat! Within a verse or two, Elijah was on the run,
fearing for his life. He was threatened not by Ahab and
his armies, not by the mighty prophets of Baal and their
revengeful families, but frightened out of his mind by a
woman. Physically, psychologically, and emotionally exhausted, he ran and ran and ran. Finally we find him
sitting in the entrance of his cave of disillusionment, his
cave of spiritual retirement in his religious mountain.

As I prepared to teach this story in my Bible study,
God found me right where I was. I mused in my heart
about how exhausted I had been feeling. Many wonderful things were happening. Great congregations. The
fire fell week after week — God's life-transforming
power evident to the watching people. The prophets of
Baal were being defeated. But, oh, how tired I was.

As I climbed my mountain to pray for rain — rivers
of living water for the spiritual deserts in men's and
women's lives around us — I looked for the rain cloud.
It came. God answered prayer every time I prayed, but
I was getting far too tired even to climb my mountain.
My Christian service was becoming mechanical. Go to
the right things, say the right words, look the right way.
Answer the same questions, battle with the long phone
calls. It was almost a treadmill of Christian activity. I
wasn't listening any more when people spoke to me. I
didn't have time to look them straight in the eyes because I was always looking past them — too impatient
even to stop for a minute. I was also extremely "remote"
at home.

It's at times like this that the snake always produces
a Jezebel: someone or some circumstance that takes you
under and you find yourself running away. Oh, you
can't run away physically, but you surely can mentally.

You can withdraw to your cave of retirement, wrap yourself in your cloak of self-pity, and complain religious complaints to the Lord.

"I've been very zealous for You, Lord! I, only I, am left!" How I love the appearance of the Lord Jesus in this story. He knows our frame, He remembers we are *dust*. When Elijah fell, his face in the ground, totally spent, the angel of the *Lord* (Jesus Himself) touched him! He said nothing — no rebuke, no command. He just touched him. Taking his overwrought servant in His arms, loving him, He provided meat and water for his needs. "Let me die," cried Elijah. "I'm no better than my fathers!" Depressed to the point of suicidal contemplations, Elijah longed to be finished with it all.

Now from God's viewpoint, this little incident must have been most frustrating. His plans had been upset. One day away from following through and finishing off Jezebel, Elijah runs away! Israel, thoroughly convinced by the miracle on Carmel, was ready for His leadership. How grateful we should be that God is never peeved and never deals with *us* as we most certainly would if *we* were God. He simply touched Elijah and patiently waited in the inner recesses of the cave to speak to His exhausted prophet.

In my exhausted state, I found I could be still and experience that "underneath and all around are the everlasting arms." God is in no hurry. We are not indispensable to His plans and purposes. He can wait. And He does. "Beware of the barrenness of a busy life," someone has said. Sometimes we are sick simply to make us learn to "rest," not only physically, but spiritually.

Once God in His goodness has given us a physical break, it's time for some company. None of us are entitled to retirement in some cozy cave where we can put up our feet on an easy rock forever. A cave in the country is no answer to our problem. There are far too many permanent Christian cave dwellers today!

Are you a Christian cave dweller? Are you living in

a cave of disillusionment? Upset with God because
Jezebel reigns in your kingdom and God just doesn't
seem to be cutting loose? Have you lost your faith? Or
is it a cave of self-righteousness? "I, only I, am left to
care in my church fellowship," you say. Or is it a cave of
self-preservation? "They seek my life to take it away!"

I suppose I have spent time in all these and many more
caves in my Christian life. But when I've had my rest
and licked my wounds and grumbled at God, my cave
insulation is never adequate enough to stop the "still
small voice."

"What doest thou here, Elijah? This is not the position for you. Go, return!" You can wrap your ears in
your mantle like Elijah did to shut out the voice, but
you'll never succeed. The only time you will be allowed
to retire is to your heavenly mansion!

Thoroughly exhausted, physically and in every other
way, I was busy settling into a cave of self-complacency.
The women's retreats were growing, and it gave me a
nice swell of pride (which, incidentally, I hastened to
call spiritual satisfaction!) to humbly tell of the growth
of the work at conventions far and near. Surely Milwaukee must feel the impact of 2,000 women. I had a
vague warning feeling about that smug statement, but being too tired to pray, I dismissed it with a careless shrug.

Walking into church the next Sunday, one of our
ushers pushed a little note into my hand. It said simply,
"Can you take a ladies' meeting at 9:00 P.M. next Sunday?" I nodded and went to my seat. The following
week as I walked into the service, I hissed at the man
who had given me the note, "Where is the meeting?"
He scribbled down an address which I didn't even
bother to look at.

That evening the snow began to fall as if it intended
to get the whole of winter over in one night! The children were more awkward than usual, and we were late
for church. We had loaned one of our cars to some missionaries, and they had gotten stuck somewhere; because

I hadn't time to get ready, I offered to drive my husband and the family to the service and then return home to prepare. My hair was an absolute mess, so I hastily stuck a large hairpiece on my head and hurried outside to the car. Arriving at church to pick up our associate pastor's wife, I skidded down the entrance slope and the car turned the wrong way around — right in the path of all the cars in the parking lot. By now the service was well underway. It was blowing like a gale, and there was nothing to do but to try and shovel my way out. As I was hardly dressed for such activity, the inevitable happened! A gust of wind — and I was left clutching my lovely hairpiece in one hand and my snow shovel in the other! I had half an hour to go before my meeting, and I had quite a drive to get there!

Tiptoeing into church, I managed to grab Gail, and we made our getaway. She tried to stick my hair back on as I drove, and she managed to produce a rather "chic" over-the-right-ear hair style!

"Where are we going?" she inquired.

Suddenly I noticed the snake all dressed up in his Sunday best sitting in the back seat. He was sniggering horribly, and I had a feeling he definitely knew something I didn't know.

All I had was the address. I had no way of knowing whether it was a church gathering, teen meeting, or what! Eventually we arrived. I looked carefully at the address again. Yes, it was right! We had arrived at the local bowling alley! The snake was already at the door eager to get a drink and try his hand. We entered and asked the man if he had seen any group of ladies around.

"Yes," he replied. "They are through that room in the back."

"Gail, I must look a freak!" I muttered. We were too late to care and headed for the back room. The door opened and we went in. Sure enough, there they were. It was a social club, and the first item on the agenda was a wine-tasting experience! The snake was completely at

home, thoroughly enjoying the whole situation. Gail and
I sat at the back politely allowing the different bottles
to pass us by. One thing comforted me — they wouldn't
notice my hair! But what on earth was I going to say?
No one took any notice of us. Maybe I was in the
wrong place, I thought hopefully.

After quite a while, a little man got up and said, "Now
then, I see our speaker has arrived. I'm afraid I don't
know anything about her." He stopped and suddenly
appeared to remember something. "Oh, yes, I do," he
countered. "I think she's got a comedy act!" The snake
was writhing around in hysterics. As I walked to the
front, my mind a complete blank, the gentleman who
had introduced me placed a nearly empty bottle of wine
in my hand. "It shall be given you in the same hour
what ye shall speak," the Lord has said. Fortunately
it was!

"O dear," I said, "the wine has run out. That happened once before in a little village called Cana. A
marriage started out on the wrong foot. Christ was there
at the wedding, but He wasn't the governor. He was
only a guest — so the wine ran out and the whole party
became flat and dull and insipid. Folks, I've come to talk
to you about Christian marriage!"

There was a completely divided audience that night.
Some were embarrassed and annoyed; a few were in-
different. But, oh, how many hungry faces turned
towards me. And suddenly I realized I'd been on my
religious mountain far too long. The cave of self-complacency needed to be left behind, and I needed to obey
the still, small voice: "What doest thou there? Go,
return — get out where the action is and reach U.S.A.
surburban women."

"But how, Lord?"

"Don't you remember?" the Lord reminded me. "Start
where you are with what you've got. Use the ladies to
reach them. Go where they are; don't expect them to
come to you."

Well, where were they? In clubs! That's where they were. But how to get in? The snake reminded me that secular clubs jealously guarded their immunity from "religious" speakers.

"There must be a way in, Lord. Show us," I prayed. We began to copy and file a list of every club in Milwaukee. We would start and visit them with a team of two ladies and ask for permission to tell about the forthcoming women's retreat and testify to what God had done for us through His Word. Then we would leave a brochure with the ladies offering them Easter and Christmas programs. Then — well — then we'd see! The Christmas and Easter readings we would use could be done by two girls with or without music or could be dramatized by a small team. The committee got to work drafting the letter.

Out of my cave — back in the world, I thanked God for my "wine-tasting" experience. At the time of this writing, the letters are on the way to their destinations, and we're climbing our mountains to pray for rain. Rain for a spiritually dry country; rain for thirsty people; life-giving rain for the dying.

I believe one day we'll see a cloud, no bigger than a man's hand, and then we'll know the showers of blessing will be well on their way!

19

Changing My Husband

"Now that you've had a chance to settle down and live together for a little while, don't you think it's time you started to change your husband?" inquired the snake one day. Now, it so happened that I'd been particularly irritated by one or two little things that morning, so I was far too willing to be drawn into a conversation with the nasty thing. I forgot Eve's lasting example and engaged in a dialogue with the enemy. "Don't you think he ought to be more organized?" the snake inquired.

"Like me?" I asked proudly.

"Yes, dear, just like you!" he replied.

Yes, I did think this would really help matters. If only I could get Stuart to change — to do things my way instead of seemingly at the last minute. The snake knew that Stuart and I were scheduled to speak at a seminar on marriage that afternoon, and I began to get increasingly uptight. My husband had still not told me what he wanted me to do for my part of the meeting. He certainly hadn't deliberately withheld the information (as the snake was trying to suggest), but for many good reasons he'd just been too hectically busy to get around to telling me.

"Tell him it's time he got prepared," the snake hissed, and before I could stop it, it was out! I received a justified sharp rebuke and in a subdued mood got into the car to go to our seminar on "marriage"!

Things were very quiet in the vehicle (except for that horrid creature chattering in the back seat). I thought hard about it all. Should a wife try to change her husband? Maybe I should change! No, I don't mean change to doing everything his way — I don't work like that; but I could certainly take a good look at my partner and, instead of bugging him, seek to help him get things done.

I noted that Stuart usually got things finished, even if some were accomplished at the last minute. The reason for this was because he was trying to do the work of three people. So, I concluded, why couldn't I just schedule *my* time to enable me to be around at these last minutes. To be available — to think ahead for him. I'd try it!

After the silence in the car had continued long enough, we began to laugh. After all, something had to be done. However could we stand up in front of all these people and talk with authority on married bliss! I thought how typical of the snake this was. He was forever slithering around our calendars noting the meetings we had and planning lots of nasty upsetting "happenings" just before we went out the door! Why didn't I see the danger signs? I'd really been on my guard every Thursday morning before my ladies' Bible class for many weeks. Invariably the children would be quite difficult,

and I would shout at them or do something that would
really give the snake the chance to point his tail. I'd
recognized the danger and had been on my guard — so
much so that the children were always happy about
Thursday mornings. They reckoned they could get
away with anything because they knew I couldn't shout
at them! But bless them, they didn't push me too hard.
They knew the meeting ended at 11:00 A.M!

The pattern was there. Before any service for the
Lord the snake would be busy seeking to wreck relationships. Sitting in the car on the way to our seminar on
Christian marriage, I thought about Ephesians 5. I had
such a nice scripturally pat talk on submission. It
sounded so right — and it was! Straight from the Word.
But could I be honest. Honesty was tough for me. The
person I had been before my conversion had taken
twenty years to submit to His Spirit. When I was first
saved and was asked a question I couldn't answer, I just
made it up! Lies! Hypocrisy!

I thought about Ananias and Sapphira. "We've given
everything," they said. They had consented together to
lie. To say their joint commitment was complete. God,
the God of Truth, knew better. Their witness impressed
no one! They were buried along with their lies. Sure,
the early Christian church remembered these two. They
remembered them for their dishonesty.

I knew we had to be honest — share our problems and
His answers. I thought about young John Mark in the
Scriptures. What a well-meaning failure he was. Shivering in the Garden of Gethsemane trying to look like an
olive tree, he failed to follow his Savior to the cross.
Later he failed Paul and Barnabas on his first missionary
trip. And yet he made it spiritually in the end. Why?
How? What happened? We aren't told specifically the
steps to his full commitment, but we do know Barnabas,
Uncle Encouragement, picked him up, and we do know
his mother believed in prayer, and we do know Peter,
perhaps the greatest influence on that young man's life,

was honest with him. Mark's gospel has sometimes been
called the gospel of Peter; i.e., Peter is believed to be the
source, and I think I know what happened to young
John Mark. I think when Peter gave him a copy of his
gospel, Mark found tremendous encouragement to go on
and find victory.

How thankful I am for the people in my life who
have been honest enough to be honest! I remembered
giving my testimony of my struggle to let Stuart be
away so much. A young evangelist's wife walked forward at the end of that meeting. (I didn't know until
four years later that she had decided to take her life
before she came to that meeting.) All she had tried to
do and be as an evangelist's wife was to her a hopeless
failure. The only talks she'd heard had been idealistic
and "everything's roses" with "Jesus talk." Sharing my
failures as well as my victories had been God's answer
to that girl's needs.

Stuart and I had a great meeting at our marriage
seminar that day. It paved the way for a youth seminar
on "Love, Courtship, and Marriage" which we were
asked to do for thousands of British teens at Spre-e 73
in London, England, the next year.

We were learning to work together. Instead of getting uptight and deciding to "change" Stuart, I decided
to change *me*, pray a lot, trust Him to give me enough
time to prepare, and paste a copy of the following study
of Ephesians in my Bible for my own instruction.

EPHESIANS 5:33 — However, let each man of you
(without exception) love his wife as [being in a sense]
his very own self; and let the wife see that she respects
and reverences her husband — that she notices him, re-
gards him, honors him, prefers him, venerates and esteems
him; and that she defers to him, praises him, and loves
and admires him exceedingly.

After reading this verse in *The Amplified Bible*, I looked
at my dictionary just to make sure I understood what
reverence really meant.

1. *Notice him* — Heed; pay attention to. Take delight in your husband. Don't ignore him.
2. *Regard him* — Gaze upon with steady significant look. Listen to; give full attention. When he comes home, don't chatter endlessly about your day; he may be impatient to get a word in about *his* day.
3. *Honor him* — Pay high respect; place in an exalted position. If you expect to be treated like a queen, you must treat him as king of his castle. Don't put him down.
4. *Prefer him* — Promote him; believe in him. Help him to believe in himself.
5. *Venerate and esteem him* — Consider worthy, appreciate and prize him. Remember that you picked him, and it doesn't say much for your good taste if you can't venerate and esteem him.
6. *Defer to him* — Make concessions in opinions and actions. Be the first to say you're sorry. Is winning your point worth a full-scale row or a "cold war"?
7. *Praise him* — Express warm approval. Don't hesitate to tell him — say it! If you don't, he may listen to another who will.
8. *Love and admire him exceedingly* — Love deeply. *Enjoy your husband!*
No man could help loving a woman like that!

20

The Pastor's Children

"And where are your children, Mrs. Briscoe?" asked a lady visiting our church.

"Oh, they're around," I answered casually.

I didn't want to point them out. Not because I was ashamed of them, but because I didn't want them to be objects of curiosity — different — "the pastor's kids." P.K.'s are supposed to be a special race. The wild ones! The kids who always fall off pedestals they never mounted. We wanted to shield them from this kind of pressure.

However, we tried to give our children a sense of pride and privilege in being part of a family whose vocation is to serve. And this they appeared to understand and accept without reluctance. Ever since our

earliest days at Capernwray in England the children had
grown up with a sense of mission. Our home was certainly our home, but its doors were always open; its
rooms, however small, were always full — and they loved
it. If, for a moment of time, no visitor or "adopted"
family member would be living with us, our eldest boy
would soon be asking, "Who's coming next? No visitors
for lunch?" Of course, they benefited, too. What a blessing our constant stream of visitors have been to our
little ones.

One student girl from Germany began to do David's
Bible reading with him. She was concerned about
his bedtime story inevitably being cut short by an
important phone call or some minor or major crisis con-
nected with the teen-age youth work for which I was
responsible. Purchasing some Scripture Union notes at
his age level, she so instilled a disciplined habit of
Scripture reading into him that he can look back to seven
years of nightly study. How grateful we are to that girl.

Sometimes the children have seen broken, marred
lives enter our home. They have watched God's trans-
forming power begin to work. They have also learned
the crippling lessons of human beings refusing to allow
His healing and have watched the resultant disintegration
of a marriage situation or life itself.

How grateful I was to my Lord for giving us these
precious teen years together with our children. We
knew that the church life would be an important part of
the help we would need. And I was well aware that God
would be using others to be a blessing to our children
in their teen years, even as we had managed to help
other people's children.

Praying about my part as their mother, I decided I
would work in their age group in the church program,
and I was able to begin the junior high work. We began
with eleven children. I discovered they loved to pray.
The first time was a bit dramatic — for them and me. I
handed a Bible to the first boy and said, "Okay, kids,

we are all going to pray aloud. When someone hands you the Bible, start praying!" Then I quickly shut my eyes, but not before I'd glimpsed their horrified faces! Everyone prayed! The next time was better, and the third meeting we discarded the Bible.

Simple Bible studies, rap groups, different approaches, a little fun and recreation. The young people loved it, and soon we were having testimony nights and five-minute talks on different topics, music nights, poetry, art, and drama and anything else that would help us all get to know the Lord better and keep full participation from the youngsters. The small rap groups helped to find out their spiritual needs, and we discovered that a lot of the printed junior high material was written to cure chicken pox when it was a case of polio that needed treating.

We began a question box, answering a few each week. "What's prematerial sex?" (He meant premarital!) "Now I'm a Christian, can I kiss a girl?" asked a bright thirteen-year-old boy. "What's hell like?" asked another. "Well, I guess hell is like being able to take one good look at God and then never being allowed to look again," answered another.

The time was always lively and interesting, and it was a great thrill to me to have my two junior highers in that group of eager learners. I found I had severely underestimated their capacity for Bible study. Many of them began to study the Navigator notes or Scripture Union material daily. They learned how to do book reviews to share with the group. Bible study materials produced for high school students were handled well by a bright minority. Our own twelve-year-old daughter took a file to church and made excellent sermon outlines and also is completing the Navigator Bible study series of twelve books. How thrilling to be their spiritual and physical mother. I had led Peter and Judy to Christ when they were very young. Now I could give them principles to build their lives upon in the vital years.

Precept upon precept, line upon line, here a little, there a little.

Peer pressure is a great influence at junior high level, and I realized it was up to me—especially in the summer months — to have "open house" all the time. To provide barbecues and swimming fun, games and overnights, inviting many of our children's Christian friends into our home circle. It's true that you can't choose your children's friends, but there are many practical ways you can surround them with Christian youngsters so they are more likely to choose their closest friends from a Christian group.

I found myself beginning to live on my knees! I asked the Holy Spirit to tell me when one of the children needed prayer. Perhaps a vulnerable moment at school, a moral danger, a physical need. Over and over again an inner "bug" would tell me to pray, and then the peace came. I knew I would have to get to heaven before I would find out all the miracle answers to those prayers. I prayed that each child would not just be "good" — you know, have enough religion to make him or her respectable. I prayed for a fully committed young life as early as possible: fullness of life, wholeness of personhood, usability by God, and a life fully set aside and sold out for Him, whether in secular society or full-time Christian service. I knew this had to be the best thing I could ever wish for my children.

Into my busy schedule I included some specific time each day where I would do "something" with each child individually. Singling them out was a real relationship-building experience. I asked each of the older children to take turns having Peter's quiet time with him and also helped to organize outreach for them at their own level.

Little teams began to be formed from their group to go to old folks' homes, orphanages, handicapped centers, and backyard Bible schools. They would write down their skills, and then we would team them up and send them forth. Some could sing or play an instrument.

Some said they wanted to talk or witness. One told us he was an excellent juggler, while another could draw while someone preached! Our children had so much head knowledge of the Scriptures, but I knew it would only be applied as they verbalized it and tried to share it with others.

I experienced many fears and discovered that "fear hath torment." The Bible also says that God hasn't given us the spirit of fear. And if God hadn't given it to us, then I knew the source. The snake! He made sure I experienced reasonable and unreasonable fear, and the only relief I found were the promises of God and perfect love, and both were rediscovered on my knees. "Perfect love casts out fear." It was on my knees that I remembered He loved my children more than I could ever love them. What was more, He reminded me I hadn't saved them, therefore I didn't have to keep them! He kept those He chose, and *no man* would be able to tear them from His grasp! I began to pray specifically and see specific answers to prayer.

Our children's spare time was completely wrapped up in the life of the church. By choice, too. How my heart thrilled as David, at fifteen, was able to go on tour with a Christian musical group. They sang and witnessed, prayed and shared, and opened up to His Spirit to take over their young lives.

When one of the children had a struggle period, I began to share the need with a few "real prayers." The results were so thrilling and encouraging. We shared some of our burdens about the church and prayed daily around the meal table for people and situations, church and school problems.

I suddenly realized that these would be the only precious years we would have to give and to enjoy, to get to know our children as *people*. I asked the Lord that I would have no regrets looking back when they were over. And I prayed that looking forward with His omniscient power He would have no regrets either where our precious children's lives were concerned.

I love Amy Carmichael's poem about her "children."
I pray it often. Amy worked among the children of
India, rescuing them from the fate of prostitution in the
heathen temples. Sometimes her children were stolen
from the mission compound. Then she could only pray:

> Father, hear us, we are praying,
> Hear the words our hearts are saying,
> We are praying for our children.
>
> Keep them from the powers of evil,
> From the secret, hidden peril,
> Father, hear us for our children.
>
> From the whirlpool that would suck them,
> From the treacherous quicksand, pluck them,
> Father, hear us for our children.
>
> From the worldling's hollow gladness,
> From the sting of faithless sadness,
> Father, Father, keep our children.
>
> Through life's troubled waters steer them,
> Through life's bitter battles cheer them,
> Father, Father, be Thou near them.
>
> Read the language of our longing,
> Read the wordless pleadings thronging,
> Holy Father, for our children.
>
> And wherever they may bide,
> Lead them Home at eventide.

21

Walkie-Talkie

In all our relationships there is a choice set before us. We can do our "duty" or we can identify. With our children we can do those things mothers do: wash their clothes, fill their stomachs, and choose the best schools for their education. I heard a lady give her testimony once, and she started off by saying, "I was a good mother to my children — but, then, so was my cat!" We can "buy" them fun; especially in America, I found much "fun" on the market. Legitimate healthy sport and exercise, occupations, and club life. We can give them everything — except ourselves!

We are too impatient to identify. And it's only when we identify that we can communicate. So many people live in the same house and play "walkie-talkie"! Our two

boys loved to play walkie-talkie. Somebody had given
them two little radio sets, and they would make sure they
never came into contact. Then they would speak a cryp-
tic message into the receiver. Just a word or two. Nothing
important — just enough to let the other know they were
in the house. Then a little phrase would come over the
air, "Over and out!"

How many of us are playing walkie-talkie with someone we live with? Maybe we don't even realize we are
doing it. We get into a remote position in a relationship
and every now and then throw out a little phrase to make
sure the other hears our voice — and then it's "over and
out" without a meaningful communication ever happening. We tuck our children up in bed and they cling to us,
asking irrelevant questions, giving us news that really is
not at all related to our adult world. "They're just putting
off the 'sleep' hour," we say impatiently as we pat them,
kiss them, tuck them up, and tell them, "No, you can't
have another glass of water!"

There came a time in my experience when I stopped
being impatient inside; I got that second glass of water
and brought it to my child, sprawled on her bed, and began to identify. I got inside her life; I listened to her
hopes, her fears, bit my tongue when she'd tell me
things I wanted to "moralize" about and sought to show
her "why not to" instead of responding with a "you're
not to." The visitors could wait. The phone call could
be made later. *Nothing* mattered in that moment of time
except my little girl. And I asked myself what I'd been
doing all these years!

Could my children be free to tell me how they'd
failed? They were the pastor's kids. They weren't
supposed to fail. If they did, would I be the one they'd
tell so I could assure them that failure made no difference to love. They wouldn't confide in me if I'd been
playing "walkie-talkie"!

What about the "boy-girl" bit? How could my son
like that little blond who obviously wasn't going to be

good for him instead of that cute red-haired deacon's child? The temptation to tell him he had to like who I liked was intense! Were he and I identifying enough to have him share his relationships with me — not ask me my opinion, but tell me his feelings, his fears and hopes. And if he wasn't asking me, I learned I wasn't to tell him. I needed to listen, pray, commit it, and let him know that *when* he got around to asking he'd get an unbiased opinion based on the principles of the Word of God, instead of an overprotective rose-tinted mother's angle on the issue!

And what about other relatives? What about my mother-in-law? Well, now, everyone knows we need to identify with our family, but no one expects us to do anything *but* play "walkie-talkie" with mother-in-law! After all, didn't the Bible say we were to "leave" our parents and cleave to our husbands? Some people take that verse as their biblical excuse for abandoning all responsibility. In fact, some women have a warmer relationship with the girl at the supermarket counter than they ever do with their own husband's mother!

Having one of the most beautiful warm relationships with my own wonderful mother certainly made me desire a similar experience with Stuart's mother. Obviously it could never be the same, but I realized right from the start the quality of our times together was of great importance.

The snake's campaigns to wreak havoc with this "special" relationship are so successful that I refuse even to give him mention in this chapter. Suffice it to say — he is very busy and usually very successful!

Visits of in-laws are usually confined to special holidays, etc., depending on distance separating the "'combatants." No, don't think that's too strong a word. After being in the pastorate and being involved in many family situations, that is the only way I can describe some of these relationships! But what about a situation that necessitates longer visits? Well, you can sit around and hope it doesn't happen to you, decide that can only work out if you are an unusual sort of person, or take a good hard look at yourself and ask the Lord just what He expects our attitude to be.

When we invited my mother-in-law to visit us for a three-month stay, I decided I needed to do just that. Where was I to look? Well, it would help if there was actually an example of a mother-in-law — daughter-in-law situation right in the Scriptures. I found the obvious one and settled down to study it. It was, of course, in the book of Ruth. Actually it is the story of a contrasted relationship: Orpah and Ruth both having the same mother-in-law and both girls having the same choice. They could identify or play "walkie-talkie."

Naomi had done a good job. For her part, she had been able to accept and love the two heathen girls her sons had chosen as their wives — girls who were different from herself. Her witness and her love had been enough to convert Ruth to the Lord Jehovah. Orpah, too, loved her mother-in-law and started out with Ruth to accompany her back to her homeland. Tragedy had struck the family and death had visited their home taking away all of their menfolk. Now they would seek a new life together in Naomi's homeland.

On the way home, Naomi stopped and, apparently feeling it was a selfish thing to take the girls with her, gave them another chance to choose. "You go your way; I'll go mine. Our customs and ways and even our Gods and the way we worship are so different — I cannot take you with me. We could never live together. There would be too many problems and conflicts." Somewhere along the road we, too, have to choose. We can go our separate ways or we can go on together. We can *try* or we can *tolerate*.

Now the crunch came. Orpah wept, kissed her mother-in-law, and left. Each agreed quite amicably to go her own way. They would play "walkie-talkie." But Ruth! She clung to Naomi and said, "Entreat me not to leave thee, or to return from following after thee: for whither thou goest, I will go; and where thou lodgest, I will lodge: thy people shall be my people, and thy God my God: Where thou diest, will I die, and there will I be buried: the Lord do so to me, and more also, if ought but death part thee and me." In effect Ruth said, "I'm going to *identify!*" A kiss is not enough if we profess to be Christians. Ruth was *determined* to go with Naomi. She simply made up her mind about the matter.

There it was. I could be an Orpah or a Ruth. Mine was the choice. I had the strangest sense of immense importance as I read those words. It's a bit dramatic, I thought. After all, mum is only coming for a three-month visit. I told the Lord I wanted to be a Ruth, not an Orpah. I saw how Ruth had honored Naomi, shared her joys and fears with her. She had placed her child within her arms to love and cherish. I realized how Naomi had surrendered her right to have Boaz for herself. "Submit yourself one to the other" was not written for husbands and wives alone!

Mother came, and we had a great time. Four weeks after her arrival, I had to take her to the hospital, only to discover that she had cancer! Three operations and nine months later, I'm thinking about the lessons of that book. Of one thing I'm sure — the only way is a "daily" Ruth identification. The daily choice is ours. I made it and I want it — and so does Naomi. Orpah wept and returned to her own country, her own kin, and her own selfishness. Ruth married Boaz. She became the richest woman in town, having a part in the line of the Lord Jesus Christ Himself. To be a Ruth means inevitable relationship with Jesus Christ, and in the end that is *all* that matters.

I love the story of Ruth. It records for us the story of Naomi and Ruth's homecoming. It says the whole city was stirred because of them. On her own confession, Naomi had gone away full; now she returned empty — except for the precious gift of the love of her daughter-in-law.

You may read this and say, "Well, I'm not as lucky as you. My mother-in-law is no Naomi!" The Bible points out that Naomi was a lonely, bitter woman. "Call me Mara," she said. "Mara" means "bitterness." Love changed all that. Ruth's overflowing love. She trusted her child into Naomi's care. She respected her advice. She never returned empty-handed at the end of the day. All that she had gathered that day she shared. She just decided to try and share her blessings. No wonder the whole city was moved.

Boaz, in testimony to Ruth, told her how people had spoken to him about all that she had done for her mother-in-law. "God will bless you for it," he said. And, of course, He always does.

Do you want to move a city? Don't plan an evangelistic campaign. Try being a Ruth!

22

Perspective

"Let's get ourselves into perspective, shall we?" said my Lord. "Never forget — you're nothing more than a little dust lady. Do you know that? 'Dust thou art, and unto dust shalt thou return.' "

I thought about that and wrote the following:

Dust cannot be *independent*. Dust is *dependent* on a supernatural force to keep it sticking together, and we are told *Who* that force is — the Bible says *by Him all things consist*. God laughs as He listens to dust talk.

Talk that says:
I don't need God.

My own self-sufficiency will keep
me from falling apart —
My own *dust mind*,
Dust abilities.
In the words of a well-known song: *I'm strong*
I'm invincible
I'm woman!

And God says: *Puff!*
And dust flies away!

A little dust person is dependent on climate, on dust
food and shelter, and on dust health.
Germs love dust. It's a lifelong battle to keep them
at bay.
God is perfect health. He has never been sick in one
moment of eternity.
But little dust people prefer to rely on bottles of dust
pills advertised on dust television. They seldom ask
the *source of health* to shine *His rays* into their dust
bodies and, if it be His will, heal their diseases.

Dust thinks it can figure out the universe, understand
all mysteries, solve all riddles, and ingeniously has
learned to manipulate atoms so it can blow up all the
other little dust people in the world.

But God loves His little dust people. They are His
idea. He wants to reconcile them to Himself so they
can discover His best. Held together by His power —
secure in His keeping — He longs to bless them so
much that He placed an ever-living spirit *within them*
and planned a resurrection body that would never
disintegrate. It would even have the ability to live
God's sort of life with Him.

God wanted to be sure the dust people understood the
plan of salvation, so He came Himself and lived in a
dust body for a time so He could tell them about His
wonderful plan *personally*.

Some dust got very angry and tried to blow Him apart, but other little men, women, and children who knew they were but dust clung to Him and acknowledged freely their absolute dependence on

The source of their being,
Creator and sustainer of their life,
Savior of their souls.

When their dust bodies were laid in dust boxes, their spirits went at once to be with Him in heaven's home.

Proud dust, watch out!
Dust thou art, and unto dust shalt thou return.
Humble dust, blessed art thou.
Dependent dust, He will not disappoint you.
One day, *glorified dust* you will be!

This little piece of dependent dust thought about that last line. "Glorified dust you will be!" And suddenly I thought of something else. On that glorious day, *there won't be a snake in my garden!*

Alleluia!